LONDON'S
ARCHITECTURAL
WALKS

JIM WATSON

Temple Church

CITY
BOOKS

CITY BOOKS • BATH • ENGLAND

Whitehall from Trafalgar Square

First published 2017
Reprinted 2018
2nd edition 2019

City Books, c/o
Survival Books Limited,
Office 169, 3 Edgar Buildings,
George Street, Bath BA1 2FJ, United Kingdom
Tel: +44 (0)01305-246283
email: info@survivalbooks.net
website: www.survivalbooks.net

British Library Cataloguing in Publication Data
A CIP record for this book is available
from the British Library.
ISBN: 978-1-913171-01-8.

Printed in India
Production managed by Jellyfish Print Solutions

Contents

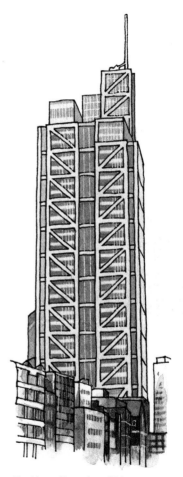

The Heron Tower from Bishopsgate

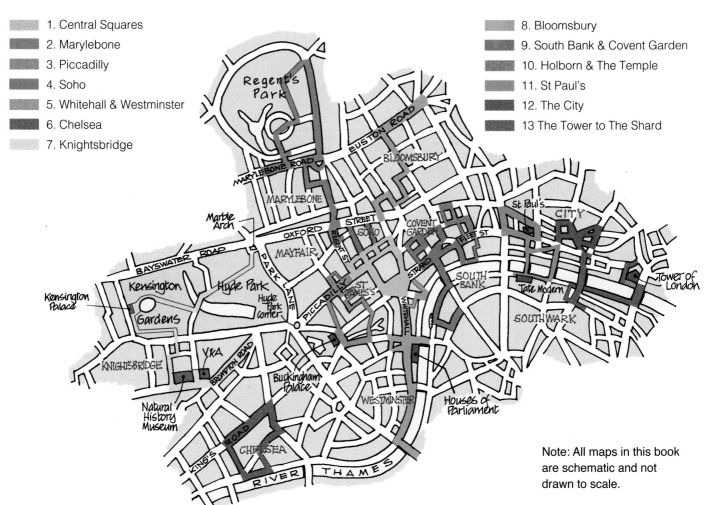

1. Central Squares
2. Marylebone
3. Piccadilly
4. Soho
5. Whitehall & Westminster
6. Chelsea
7. Knightsbridge

8. Bloomsbury
9. South Bank & Covent Garden
10. Holborn & The Temple
11. St Paul's
12. The City
13 The Tower to The Shard

Regent's Park

MARYLEBONE ROAD

EUSTON ROAD

BLOOMSBURY

MARYLEBONE

St Paul's

CITY

Marble Arch

OXFORD STREET

SOHO

COVENT GARDEN

FLEET ST

BAYSWATER ROAD

MAYFAIR

REGENT ST

STRAND

SOUTH BANK

Tower of London

Kensington

Hyde Park

PARK LANE

PICCADILLY

ST. JAMES'S

Tate Modern

Kensington Palace

Gardens

Hyde Park Corner

WHITEHALL

SOUTHWARK

V.&.A.

BROMPTON ROAD

Buckingham Palace

Knightsbridge

Natural History Museum

KING'S ROAD

Westminster

Houses of Parliament

CHELSEA

RIVER THAMES

Note: All maps in this book are schematic and not drawn to scale.

Introduction

London is one of the world's great cities, steeped in two thousand years of history and rich in culture, architecture and agreeable surprises.

This series of walks will take you to many of the famous landmarks, which are relatively close to each other so no route exceeds four miles in length. Each begins and ends at an underground station, the circular walks at the same station.

London is architecturally diverse. A third of the city was destroyed in the Great Fire of 1666, including the old St Paul's Cathedral, but subsequently rebuilt on the old medieval street plan giving architects such as Christopher Wren the opportunity to show their genius. *London's Architectural Walks* will take you to the architectural hotspot of the City where London was founded in Roman times, show you the artistic legacy of Chelsea and the great museums of Bloomsbury and Knightsbridge. Also included are the bastions of royal and political power, the heart of the English legal system, plus Georgian squares, Victorian railways and John Nash's blissful terraces.

The River Thames provides an enduring backdrop to the architecture as we visit the South Bank cultural area, the ancient Tower of London, soaked in history, and Pugin's masterpiece, the Houses of Parliament. You'll cross iconic bridges, including Tower Bridge and the famous 'wobbly' Millennium Bridge. We'll also take in the tranquility of ancient churches and the wonderful Royal Parks, expansive and free for everyone to enjoy.

London's skyline has seen dramatic changes in recent years; the burgeoning growth of skyscrapers bring a constant source of amazement, now with the glittering Shard towering over all.

By far the best way to enjoy all these riches is on foot. However, walking in central London is not like country walking. The crowds, traffic and less than pure air can be tiring and paving stones are a lot harder on the feet than grass. Take your time; there's plenty of places to rest and usually a plethora of refuelling stops.

The pleasures of London are many and varied but few are such good value for money as just looking. Many of these buildings have magnificent interiors and house wonderful treasures; but often it's sufficient to just stand outside and marvel at the human creativity, skill and tenacity that went into their construction.

I hope you enjoy this book and the buildings that inspired it. May they stimulate you as much as they did me while I was drawing and writing about them.

Jim Watson

Rugby, June 2019

What is this life if, full of care,
we have no time to stand and stare?
W.H. Davis

Shop sign,
Bloomsbury

WALK 1

The Central Squares

Places of interest

1. Piccadilly Circus
2. Eros
3. Horses of Helios
4. Leicester Square
5. Shakespeare statue
6. Odeon Cinema
7. National Portrait Gallery
8. Edith Cavell statue
9. St Martin-in-the-Fields
10. Charing Cross Station
11. Eleanor Cross
12. Trafalgar Square
13. National Gallery
14. Nelson's Column
15. Charles I statue
16. Admiralty Arch
17. Canada House
18. Institute of Directors
19. Royal Opera House Arcade
20. Her Majesty's Theatre
21. Theatre Royal, Haymarket

START & FINISH
Piccadilly Circus

This circular walk takes you to London's three central squares, with a couple of interesting detours. They each have their own diverse character. Piccadilly is brash, touristy, busy by day and night, a meeting place for four main highways and people from all over the world. The famous statue of Eros in the square was for years the best-known symbol of London. It's said that if you wait here long enough, someone you know will turn up.

In contrast, pedestrianised Leicester Square is quieter – except when there's a glitzy film premiere showing – and has a restful little park at the centre. The buildings are fairly unremarkable but have housed some notable residents.

Trafalgar Square, the largest of the three, is the most stately, has the best architecture and some of the city's most iconic landmarks including the National Gallery, the National Portrait Gallery, St Martin-in-the-Fields and Nelson's Column.

START & FINISH: Piccadilly Circus tube station.
LENGTH: 1.5 miles approx. Broad streets and traffic-free areas. No steep hills or steps. Expect crowds.
REFRESHMENTS: Fast food outlets and coffee shops aplenty. National Gallery café & restaurant. Portrait Gallery restaurant & bar. St Martin-in-the-Fields Crypt café.

The Quadrant on Regent Street

The Walk

❶ **Piccadilly Circus** – from the Latin meaning 'circle'– was developed in 1819, part of the Prince Regent's royal processional route through the capital. Designed by John Nash, it was to run from an open hunting ground on the northern edge of the city, now Regent's Park, to the prince's palace, Carlton House, in Waterloo Place (walk 3).

Nash's glorious terraces alongside the park survive (walk 2), as do his memorable designs of Park Crescent and Carlton House Terrace (walk 3). The Nash buildings on Regent Street have been replaced, but the beautiful curve of the Quadrant, where the street enters Piccadilly Circus from the north, can still be admired.

The famous statue of ❷ **Eros** tops a memorial fountain, erected in 1892-93 to commemorate Lord Shaftesbury, a Victorian politician and philanthropist. This is a busy road junction and traffic used to circulate around the fountain, but in a major redesign in the 1980s it was moved to the large paved area on the south side.

7

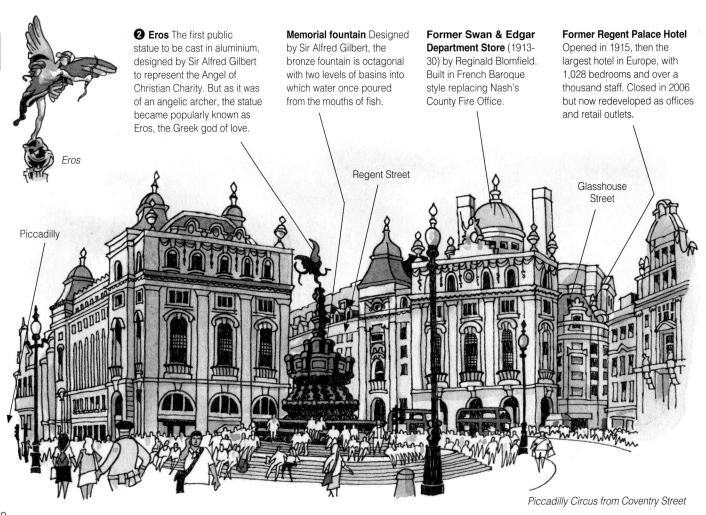

Eros

❷ **Eros** The first public statue to be cast in aluminium, designed by Sir Alfred Gilbert to represent the Angel of Christian Charity. But as it was of an angelic archer, the statue became popularly known as Eros, the Greek god of love.

Memorial fountain Designed by Sir Alfred Gilbert, the bronze fountain is octagonal with two levels of basins into which water once poured from the mouths of fish.

Former Swan & Edgar Department Store (1913-30) by Reginald Blomfield. Built in French Baroque style replacing Nash's County Fire Office.

Former Regent Palace Hotel Opened in 1915, then the largest hotel in Europe, with 1,028 bedrooms and over a thousand staff. Closed in 2006 but now redeveloped as offices and retail outlets.

Regent Street

Glasshouse Street

Piccadilly

Piccadilly Circus from Coventry Street

Leave Piccadilly Circus along Coventry Street, pausing at the corner of the Caffé Concerto building to admire the **❸ Horses of Helios** (Greek god of the sun), a 1992 bronze sculpture by Rudy Weller of four prancing horses.

Continue past various theatres and the Trocadero which was built as a restaurant in 1896 and has had numerous entertainment guises since. Cross the southern end of Wardour Street, from where there's a distant view of Chinatown, into a traffic-free section. Pass the largest Lego store in the world on your right to enter Leicester Square at its northwest corner.

The Horses of Helios

Advertising signs The first electric ads appeared here in 1910, using incandescent light bulbs. These were replaced by neon and moving signs, while the 2000s saw a gradual move to LED screen displays. The multi-screens were replaced by a single digital screen in 2017.

London Pavilion An early music hall built in 1885 to replace an older one. Converted to a cinema in 1934 and rebuilt as a shopping arcade in 1986, preserving the original façade, outer walls and roof.

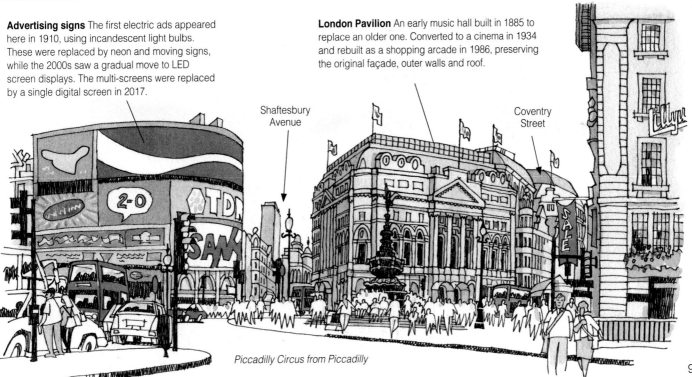

Shaftesbury Avenue

Coventry Street

Piccadilly Circus from Piccadilly

9

Now the centre of London's cinema land and prime location for glitzy film premieres, ❹ **Leicester Square** was laid out in 1670 as a gentrified residential area with famous tenants including the then Prince of Wales and artists William Hogarth and Joshua Reynolds.

The area drifted downmarket during the 18th century and by the 19th the small park in the centre, which was originally called Lammas Land, had become rundown. A restoration by Albert Grant MP in the 1870s installed four statues of famous residents but they were removed during a later restoration in the 1990s.

The square has been a centre of popular entertainment for over a century, first with music halls and now a plethora of clubs, casinos and cinemas. It was pedestrianised in the 1980s and refurbished for the 2012 London Olympics at a cost of £15 million. The TKTS booth, the official outlet to buy discount theatre tickets, has been here since 1980.

The central park in Leicester Square

The TKTS booth

A marble statue of ❺ **William Shakespeare** was installed at the centre of the park in a 19th-century restoration. Positioned above a fountain with four dolphins which used to spout water, it's by Giovanni Fontana, a copy of the memorial by Peter Scheemakers in Westminster Abbey.

Shakespeare looks rather pensive on his plinth. Perhaps he feels out of place amongst these film folk. Maybe he'd be happier in a more appropriate setting, – the Globe Theatre by the Thames perhaps?

Shakespeare statue

The Odeon cinema

Several theatres were established in the square during the 19th century, some later converted to cinemas. The distinctive 1930s Art Deco tower of the ❻ **Odeon**, which seats over 1,600 people, dominates the east side. The Empire opened in 1960, the largest cinema in the square until 2013 when it was subdivided to make space for an IMAX screen. The state of the art Vue Cinema, just off the square in Cranbourn Street, has nine screens, including three 3D screens, and can seat 2,400 people.

The Hippodrome Casino next door was built in 1900 as a venue for circus and variety acts. It's had many uses since, most famously in the 1980s as the Talk of the Town nightclub.

Chaplin statue

The bronze statue of film legend Charlie Chaplin by John Doubleday was unveiled in the central park in 1981. Chaplin is wearing his famous tramp outfit and (unlike Shakespeare) looks perfectly at home in this setting. He was removed during the square's makeover but returned to his rightful place in April 2016.

Chaplin was born into poverty in Walworth, Southeast London in 1889 but found huge fame in the USA as a comic actor, director and producer during the silent film era of the early 1900s. Widely regarded as a towering figure in the history of film, he died in Switzerland in 1977 at the age of 88.

Leave Leicester Square along Irving Street near the TKTS booth, which leads to a small open area opposite the Garrick Theatre in Charing Cross Road.

Vue Cinema and the Hippodrome

The **❼ National Portrait Gallery** is the building on your right. A statue of Sir Henry Irving, the great Victorian actor-manager, stands outside on a small green area. The statue, by Thomas Brock, was erected in 1910, paid for by a group of actors and people from the theatre world.

Sweep right to the Portrait Gallery entrance. Opened in 1896, it was designed by Ewan Christian and Dixon Jones in Italian Renaissance style with round-headed windows. The gallery displays portraits of figures from history dating back to the 14th century. A major overhaul during 1994-2000 established a gallery extension, improved visitor facilities and added a rooftop restaurant with fabulous views from 28m (92ft) above the square.

Edith Cavell statue

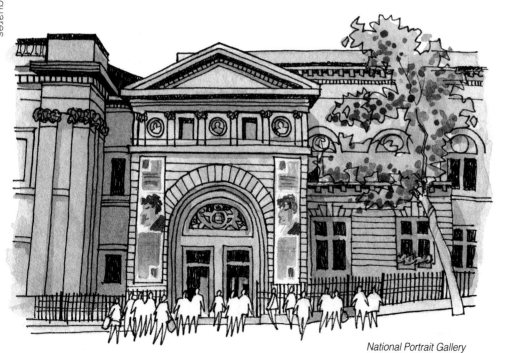

National Portrait Gallery

A striking statue across the road in St Martin's Place commemorates **❽ Edith Cavell**, a British nurse who was shot by the Germans for helping allied troops escape during the First World War.

Further along is **❾ St Martin-in-the-Fields**, designed by James Gibbs and built in 1721-6 on the site of an earlier 11th century church. With its rectangular design, portico and Baroque steeple, it inspired the design of numerous colonial churches worldwide, most notably in America and Ireland. The interior is also noteworthy with huge columns and a balcony to three sides.

London Coliseum Theatre Opened in 1904, by Frank Matcham who also designed the Palladium.

St Martin-in-the-Fields

Duke of York Theatre

St Martin's Lane

A short detour between St Martin-in-the-Fields and its award-winning café takes you onto the Strand opposite ❿ **Charing Cross Station** and Hotel, completed in 1864 when it was fashionable to build a fine-looking building in front of a train station.

Designed by E.M. Barry, the hotel is decorated with Renaissance motifs and two brightly painted galleries above the station entrances. Two upper storeys have since been added to the original design and in a radical development in 1990 a modern office and shopping complex, Embankment Place, was built over the station platforms.

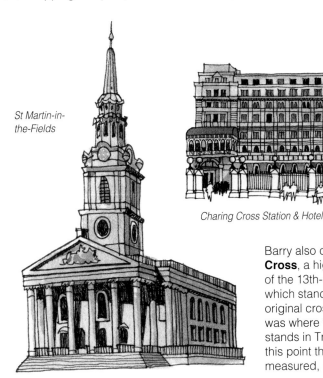

St Martin-in-the-Fields

Charing Cross Station & Hotel

Stretching north from St Martin's Place, St Martin's Lane is an interesting, narrow street of restaurants, cafés and theatres, most notably the London Coliseum, home of the English National Opera since 1974.

Barry also designed the ⓫ **Eleanor Cross**, a highly decorated replica of the 13th-century Whitehall Cross, which stands outside the station. The original cross, demolished in 1647, was where the statue of Charles I now stands in Trafalgar Square. It's from this point that distances in London are measured, not from the replica.

From Duncannon Street cross Charing Cross Road to the National Gallery and turn left to walk around the square in a clockwise direction.

You will soon come across a small round stone building with a lamp on top. This was once Britain's smallest police station, built in 1826, with its own phone line to police HQ, installed in 1926. It no longer helps the modern police with their enquiries.

Continue beyond Nelson's Column and cross the road to a traffic island where there's a grandiose statue of ⓯ **Charles I** (1600-49), glaring defiantly down Whitehall to the scene of his execution outside the Banqueting Hall (walk 5). The memorial, commissioned in 1633, is by the French sculptor, Hubert Le Suer. After years of being buried in a Holborn garden to escape being melted down, the statue has stood here, the official centre of London, since 1947.

Charles I statue

⓬ **Trafalgar Square** is named after Lord Nelson's victory in the Battle of Trafalgar in 1805 which cost him his life. Part of John Nash's grand plan for London, the square was conceived as an open space looking down Whitehall. Most of the construction was done during the 1830s but the surrounding buildings developed over the years with no overall master plan – much like the city of London itself.

The fourth plinth Designed to carry a statue of William IV but the money ran out. It remained empty until 1999 when it was decided to use the plinth to display a series of contemporary artworks which have delighted, amused and shocked the crowds ever since.

⓭ **National Gallery** Designed in neo-Classical style by William Wilkins and built during 1832-38. Houses one of the world's great collections of over 2,300 Western European paintings from the 13th century Early Renaissance to the 19th century Impressionists.

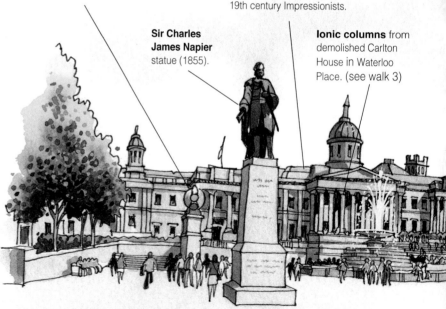

Sir Charles James Napier statue (1855).

Ionic columns from demolished Carlton House in Waterloo Place. (see walk 3)

Traffic used to cross in front of the National Gallery but since it was rerouted the square is now a completely pedestrianised, open area. Despite its regal character, the square is mostly a venue for rallies, political meetings and sales campaigns, rather than state or royal occasions.

⑭ Nelson's Column dominates the square and commemorates Admiral Lord Nelson, Britain's most famous sea lord who died heroically during his victory at the Battle of Trafalgar in 1805. Dating from 1843, the 46m (151ft) high column of Dartmoor granite is guarded by Edward Landseer's four bronze lions – much-loved, especially by climbing children – which were added 25 years later, due it is said to the artist's difficulty in creating a satisfactory lion likeness. It was worth the wait.

South Africa House Built in the 1930s on the site of a derelict hotel. Was a target for protests against racial segregation during the 1980s. In 2001, Nelson Mandela appeared on the balcony to mark the seventh anniversary of the end of the Apartheid system.

Four bronze panels Cast from captured French guns, depicting Nelson's four great victories.

St Martin-in-the-Fields

London Coliseum

George IV statue 1840s

Fountains designed by Edwin Lutyens in 1939

The Strand

Northumberland Avenue

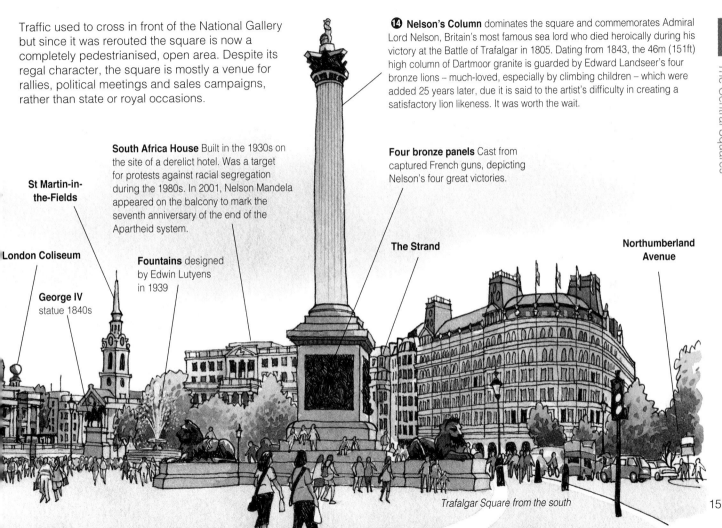

Trafalgar Square from the south

15

Across the road junction in front of the Charles I statue stands the great Portland stone edifice of ⓰ **Admiralty Arch**, built as a tribute by King Edward VII in memory of his mother, Queen Victoria. Designed by Austin Webb and built 1906-11, the arch completed the development of the Mall and St James's Park begun in the 1660s.

Traffic can only use the two outer arches, the central one being reserved for royal processions. Once the residence of the First Sea Lord and used by the Admiralty, the arch housed government offices until it was sold in 2012 for redevelopment as a luxury hotel, restaurant and apartments.

Latin inscription 'In the tenth year of King Edward VII, to Queen Victoria, from her most grateful citizens, 1910'.

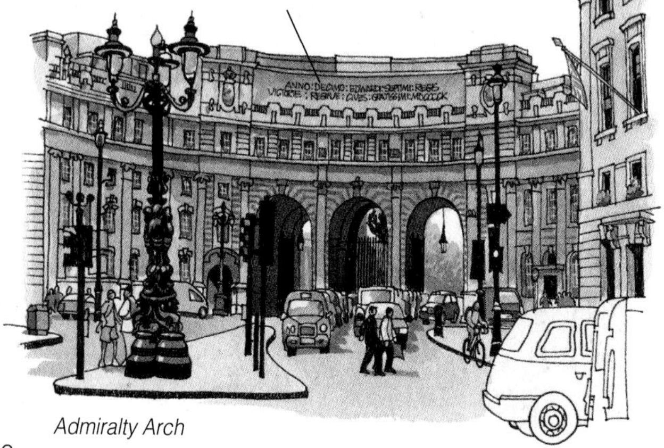

Admiralty Arch

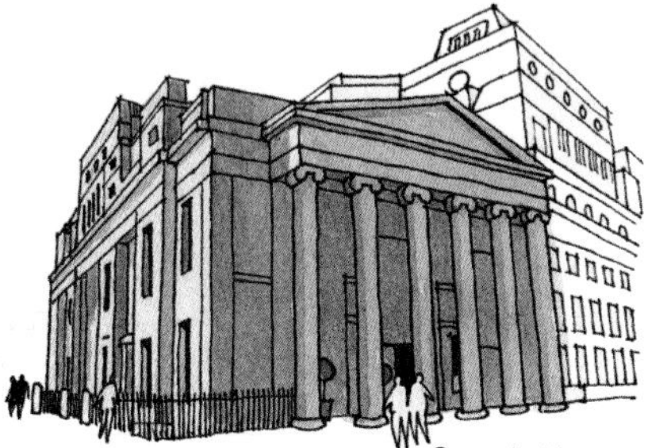

Canada House

Occupying most of the west side of the square, ⓱ **Canada House** was built between 1822-25 in Greek Revival style by Robert Smirke, who also designed the British Museum. Originally it was two buildings occupied by the Royal College of Physicians and the Union Club. Acquired by the Canadian government in 1923, the exterior was remodelled to achieve a more unified appearance.

The route leaves Trafalgar Square at its north-western corner, turning sharply past the Sainsbury extension to the National Galley into Pall Mall East. The extension, funded by the supermarket family, has a functional look about it but houses a fabulous collection of Renaissance paintings and mounts blockbuster exhibitions.

Just beyond the junction with the Haymarket the sunny stucco of the ⓲ **Institute of Directors** building comes into view on the left-hand side of Pall Mall East. Originally the United Services Club, it was built in 1827 to a design by John Nash and remodelled by his assistant Decimus Burton. It's another of Nash's production line of neo-Classical designs, this one a mixture of orders with Roman Doric prominent for the entrance porch.

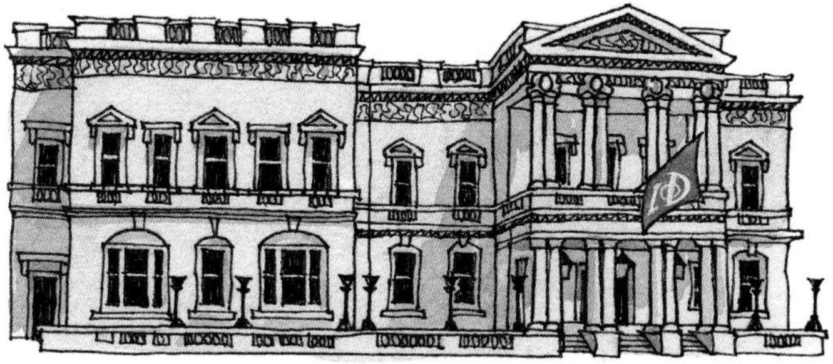

Institute of Directors

Across Pall Mall East is another of Nash's creations, the **⑲ Royal Opera Arcade**, the oldest of London's five 19th-century shopping arcades, built in 1816-18. Originally, it was the entrance to the Haymarket Opera House which was decimated by fire in 1867. The arcade survived and now houses 18 small shops, set either side of the colonnade.

Royal Opera Arcade

Walk through the arcade and turn right along Charles I Street to the Haymarket where **⑳ Her Majesty's Theatre** looms dramatically on the corner. Designed by Charles J. Phipps and opened in 1897, it replaces the Haymarket Opera House, demolished in 1891. Built in French Renaissance style, it looks remarkably like a traditional grand opera house, but as the London opera scene had now moved to Covent Garden, Her Majesty's instead staged spectacular productions of Shakespeare and other classical works. With a large stage and a seating capacity of 1,216, it has more recently been the venue for large-scale musicals. *The Phantom of the Opera* has run here since 1986 in a house well-suited for retelling Gothic tales.

Across the Haymarket is London's oldest theatre, the **㉑ Theatre Royal**. Designed by John Nash in 1831, he moved the location from further up the street so the grand portico of six Corinthian columns could be best seen from St James's Square (walk 3). The interior has been updated but much of the stage machinery is original.

A stroll to the top of the Haymarket and a left turn returns you to the end of the walk in Piccadilly Circus. Have a sit down on the steps of Eros. Everyone else does.

Royal Opera
Arcade exit

Theatre Royal, Haymarket

Her Majesty's Theatre

Marylebone

Places of interest

1. Chilton Court
2. Madame Tussauds
3. St Mary's Parish Church
4. Royal Academy of Music
5. The Regent's Park
6. Queen Mary's Gardens
7. Gloucester Gate
8. Cumberland Terrace
9. Chester Terrace
10. Royal College of Physicians
11. Park Crescent
12. Harley Street
13. Royal Institute of British Architects
14. Langham Hotel
15. Broadcasting House
16. All Soul's Church
17. Oxford Circus
18. Liberty
19. Palladium House
20. London Palladium

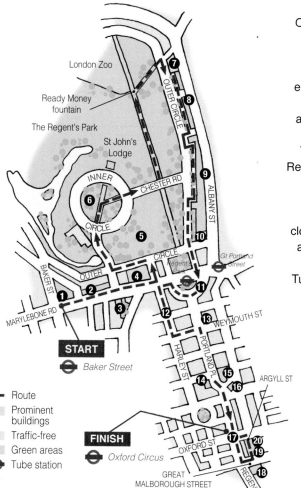

— Route

▒ Prominent buildings

▒ Traffic-free

▒ Green areas

⊖ Tube station

Originally a medieval village on the outskirts of London, Marylebone's orderly grid of streets was laid out in the 19th century by its royal landowners to build prestigious housing, enhance the area and swell the Crown coffers. The Prince Regent's creation of the park attracted professional people, making it one of London's most affluent areas.

This walk takes you from peaceful, semi-rural Regent's Park to the hustle and bustle of Oxford Circus, the junction of London's two main shopping streets and the busiest pedestrian crossing in the city. You'll be rewarded with close-ups of John Nash's breathtaking terraces and streets lined with Regency houses. There are also the London landmarks of Madame Tussauds, Broadcasting House, Liberty and All Souls Church. The architecture is varied and interesting – with some surprises.

START: Baker Street tube station.
FINISH: Oxford Circus tube station.
LENGTH: 2.75 miles approx. Parkland and broad streets. No steps. Crowds in Regent Street.
REFRESHMENTS: RIBA restaurant and café. Plenty in Regent Street.

Chilton Court

The Walk

Take the Baker Street exit out of Baker Street station and turn left along Marylebone Road. It's a busy highway, the northern boundary of the city until the 19th century development.

The huge building you have just come out of is worthy of note. The tube station was designed by Charles Walter Clarke, who worked for the Metropolitan Railway and whose headquarters it became. **❶ Chilton Court**, a large and luxurious block of apartments was built over the station in the 1920s.

Beyond Chilton Court you face two of London's most unlovely buildings. The Planetarium, opened in 1958, displayed night skies and planets projected on the inside of the landmark dome to audiences of 330. It closed in 2006 and is now part of **❷ Madame Tussauds**, a major London tourist attraction displaying waxworks of famous people.

Marie Tussaud transported her figures from France in 1802 and exhibited them around the country until 1835. She settled in Baker Street and in 1880, 30 years after her death, the exhibition was installed in this building.

Further along, the vista improves with the first glimpses of the Nash buildings around the entrance to Regent's Park.

Across the road and set back from the traffic is **❸ St Mary's Parish Church**. Designed by Thomas Hardwick, the large stately building was consecrated in 1817. The poets, Robert Browning and Elizabeth Barrett were married here in 1846 after she eloped from her strict family home in nearby Wimpole Street

Madame Tussauds and the former Planetarium dome

St Mary's Parish Church

Continue along the left of Marylebone Road and cross York Gate. The neat and tidy John Nash building on your left is the museum of the ❹ **Royal Academy of Music**, founded in 1774, England's first music academy. Next door is the Academy's main premises, dating from 1911 and designed by Ernest George with its own semi-subterranean concert hall. It's rather hidden by trees these days but still an impressive building.

The Royal Academy of Music

The Royal Academy of Music Museum

Turn left down narrow Macfarren Place alongside the Academy, then left again behind York Terrace East, one half of Nash's long terrace arrangement, built in 1824-6 and centred around the York Gate entrance to Regent's Park. Turn right to cross Ulster Terrace, but before going into the park look left to see how beautifully the two ends of Nash's York Terraces frame St Mary's church across Marylebone Road.

Beginning in 1817, John Nash, with the encouragement of the spendthrift Prince Regent, turned an area of heathland into Regent's Park, part of the grandest (and only) town-planning scheme central London has seen.

Properly named ❺ **The Regent's Park**, Nash's big idea was that it would be a garden suburb, the setting for 56 villas in a variety of classical styles with a royal palace at the centre. Only eight villas were actually built with three surviving around the edge of the Inner Circle. The Crown Estates who owned the land vetoed the building of the palace and 48 villas, worried about the cost of Nash's grand plan which stretched south to what is now Buckingham Palace.

St John's Lodge - one of Nash's surviving villas

Head into the park, crossing York Bridge over the boating lake. When you reach the Inner Circle road keep straight on through the ornamental gates into ❻ **Queen Mary's Gardens**. The Inner Circle and Chester Road are open to vehicles but the rest of the many pathways are traffic-free.

Queen Mary's Gardens, completed in 1934, are world famous for their large collection of more than 12,000 roses, in 400 varieties. This is a lovely area to wander around enjoying the gardens and general restful ambience.

Follow the signs out of the gardens and cross the Inner Circle road onto the left side of Chester Road. At the Espresso Bar turn left onto Broad Walk which takes you to the ornate Ready Money drinking fountain, named after the nick-name of Sir Cowasjee Jehangir, a Parsee industrialist who donated it in 1896.

By now the animals in nearby London Zoo will probably be making themselves heard. The zoo, opened in 1828, is a major research and conservation centre and one of London's biggest tourist attractions.

Cumberland Terrace

Queen Mary's Gardens

Angle right from the fountain onto a pathway heading to the far side of the palatial Nash terraces that you may have already seen through the trees. Leave the park and cross the Outer Circle road.

Turn right and walk along the left of the Outer Circle. Gloucester Lodge is on your left. Though mostly hidden behind trees, it's unmistakably a Nash creation, a pleasingly symmetrical house with a portico and fluted columns.

Further along at ❼ **Gloucester Gate**, Nash was really getting into his stride with a terrace of 11 houses, built in 1827, with huge pilasters and massive columns supporting decorated porticoes adorned with classical sculptures.

Turn off the Outer Circle road at Cumberland and Chester Terraces for a walk close to these magnificent stucco walls. This is serious architecture, elegant, solemn and overpowering, designed so the Prince could see it from his never-built palace.

Cumberland Terrace

Chester Terrace

❽ Cumberland Terrace, built 1826-7, grandest and most elaborate of all the 11 Regent's Park terraces, is 244m (800ft) long with a temple block at the centre. An enormous pediment, second largest in England at the time (to St Paul's), is supported by ten Corinthian columns. Exuberant sculptures by J.G. Bubb are set off beautifully by what could be described as 'Wedgwood blue'. On either side are symmetrical terraces with pavilions and detached triumphal arches.

❾ Chester Terrace dates from 1825, designed by Decimus Burton with John Nash as overseer. Nash is said to have disliked Burton's design and tried to have the terrace demolished. It has the longest unbroken façade in the park stretching for 287m (940ft) with 99 bays symmetrically arranged around a central section of seven bays. Projecting wings at each end are connected to the main building by triumphal arches. Name boards across the tops are the only ostentatious flourish.

Cumberland Terrace

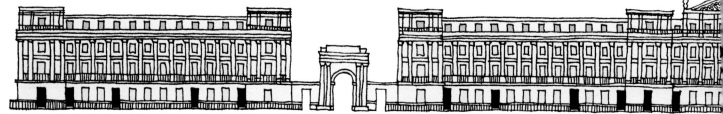

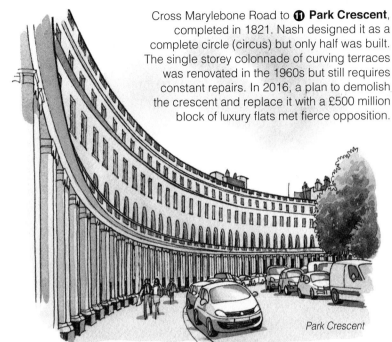

Cross Marylebone Road to ⑪ **Park Crescent**, completed in 1821. Nash designed it as a complete circle (circus) but only half was built. The single storey colonnade of curving terraces was renovated in the 1960s but still requires constant repairs. In 2016, a plan to demolish the crescent and replace it with a £500 million block of luxury flats met fierce opposition.

Royal College of Physicians

Walk on to the end of the Outer Circle road where you'll find the ⑩ **Royal College of Physicians**, built in 1960-4 to a design by Sir Denys Lasdun, whose use of mosaic clad concrete has been duplicated on many public buildings since. It's Grade 1 listed and a surprising contemporary addition amongst all the 19th-century magnificence.

Park Crescent

Walk around the crescent back into Marylebone Road. Turn left into **⑫ Harley Street,** famous for its doctors and health specialists. Fine Georgian houses line the street which has an air of hushed order – not unlike a doctor's waiting room. The doorways are varied and handsome, some so wide you might think obesity was the speciality practised inside.

Turn left along Weymouth Street with the **⑬ Royal Institute of British Architects** in Portland Place straight ahead. Built in 1932-4 and designed by Grey Wornun, its crisply cut Portland stone is obviously modern in design but in perfect harmony with the surroundings.

Bas-relief sculptures are by Edward Bainbridge Copnall and the massive cast bronze front doors, each weighing 1.5 tons, are adorned with reliefs depicting London buildings and the River Thames.

With an architectural bookshop, a fine restaurant in stunning designer surroundings, an inexpensive set menu, a café and a bar, this is a place where anyone interested in architecture should spend some time.

Beyond the Institute, there's a distant view of the BT Tower, built in 1961-65 to a design by Eric Bedford. It's part office block, part telecommunications mast.

At 190m (620ft) high it was the tallest building in London until the 1980s. A circular restaurant at the top used to be the place to be seen dining but it was closed in 1980 amid security concerns.

Harley Street doorways

BT Tower

The Royal Institute of British Architects

Stay on the left-hand side of Portland Place, and head for the Langham Hotel at the end.

Portland Place was laid out by the Adam brothers in 1773. At 34m (110ft) it's broad enough for two lanes of modern traffic either side of a central line of trees. The road was also already grand enough for John Nash to incorporate into his royal route.

A fine Adam building, Foley House, was demolished in 1864 to make way for the huge ⓮ **Langham Hotel**, creating the curious dog leg connection with Regent Street. Opened in 1865, the Langham was London's finest hotel, with Mark Twain and Oscar Wilde among its illustrious guests. After a £90 million refurbishment in 2009 the Langham now boasts 380 rooms and all the requisites of a modern five-star hotel.

Across the street from the Langham, which once housed the BBC record library, is ⓯ **Broadcasting House**, built for the BBC in 1931 as a suitably modern Art Deco headquarters for a ground-breaking broadcasting institution. The façade of the building curves with the street and is dominated by Eric Gill's stylised relief of Prospero and Ariel (Shakespeare's invisible spirit of the air). In a major consolidation completed in 2005 a new glass-fronted east wing was added at a reported cost of £1.04 billion.

Equally iconic to Broadcasting House, is ⓰ **All Souls Church**, built 1822-24 to a John Nash design, standing at an awkward angle nearby. It features an unusual circular portico and pillars of Ionic order. On top is a smaller version of itself with a slender spire, much ridiculed at the time. His only London church, it's Nash at his most whimsical.

Langham Hotel

John Nash (1752-1835) From a bust in the portico of All Souls

Broadcasting House & All Souls Church

Regent Street

Turn left into Great Marlborough Street with the magnificent **⓲ Liberty Department Store** opposite. Arthur Lasenby Liberty opened his first shop on Regent Street in 1875, selling oriental silks and objets d'art from Japan.

The present mock Tudor building was built specifically to house the store in 1925. Liberty is one of the leading destination stores in London, a wonderful emporium where the latest fashions sit alongside design classics.

Liberty store

Continue along the left-hand side of Regent Street to **⓱ Oxford Circus**, where it crosses Oxford Street, one of the busiest road junctions in the world. A project completed in 2009 costing £5 million relieved some of the area's traffic congestion but it's still a lively place. Cross Oxford Street (with care!) and carry on along Regent Street.

There's nothing left of Nash's sweeping architecture but the street still has a grand air about it with a succession of imposing buildings housing many flag-ship retailers. Among them, at number 235, is the Apple Store, mecca of today's techy generation.

The top tier detail

Palladium House

The Palladium Theatre

Further along pedestrianised Argyll Street there's London's most famous variety theatre, the 2,286 seater ❷⓿ **London Palladium**, opened in 1910. The architect was Frank Matcham who also designed the Hackney Empire, the London Coliseum and the Victoria Palace. Between 1955-67 it was the venue for the top-rated ITV show *Sunday Night at the London Palladium*, broadcast live across the nation every week and featuring top UK and American acts.

Standing on the corner of Argyll Street is a building that's unlike any other in the area. This is ❶⓿ **Palladium House**, designed by an American architect, Raymond Hood, and built in 1928. It's basically a large shiny black cube of black granite, with all six storeys punctuated by simple windows, regularly spaced. The top tiers are decorated with floral tiles and a piping of inlaid gilt. It's flashy, yet sophisticated, currently with a spaghetti house at street level.

Continue along Argyll Street to rejoin the crowds at Oxford Circus, where the walk ends.

WALK 3

Piccadilly & St James's

Places of interest

1. Hatchards bookshop
2. Fortnum & Mason
3. Royal Academy
4. Burlington Arcade
5. Ritz Hotel
6. Green Park
7. Buckingham Palace
8. Queen Anne's Gate
9. The Two Chairmen
10. St James's Park
11. Carlton House Terrace
12. Duke of York statue
13. The Athenaeum
14. Waterloo Place
15. Guards Crimean War Memorial
16. Travellers Club
17. Reform Club
18. Royal Automobile Club
19. Schomberg House
20. St James's Palace
21. Berry Bros & Rudd
22. James Lock & Co
23. St James's Square
24. St James's Church
25. Jermyn Street
26. White's

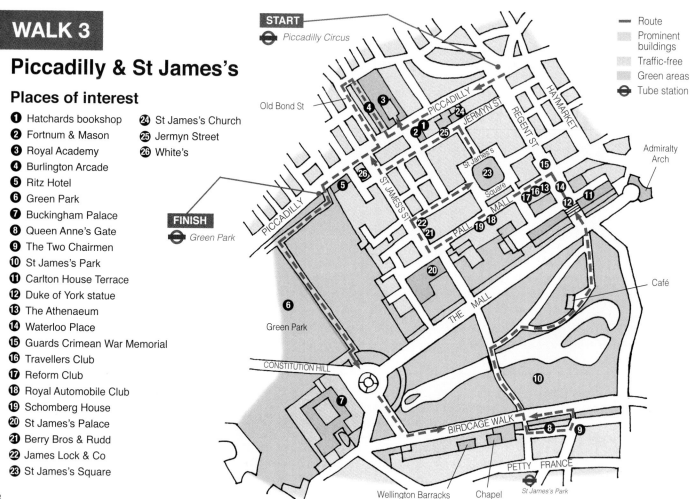

START
Piccadilly Circus

Route
Prominent buildings
Traffic-free
Green areas
Tube station

Old Bond St

PICCADILLY
JERMYN ST
REGENT ST
HAYMARKET

Admiralty Arch

St James's Square

FINISH
Green Park

PICCADILLY

PALL MALL

THE MALL

Café

Green Park

CONSTITUTION HILL

BIRDCAGE WALK

PETTY FRANCE

St James's Park

Wellington Barracks   Chapel

A main road since medieval times, Piccadilly is the main artery through the West End. The name comes from ruffs or pickadills worn by 17th-century dandies.

St James's has been one of London's most exclusive residential enclaves since it was first developed in the 1660s.

This absorbing tour of the bastions of English aristocracy takes you along high-class shopping streets, to royal palaces and parks, a fine square and the culmination of John Nash's grand plan for Regency London.

You will also enter the time-warp territory of the English male establishment: gentlemen's clubs, bespoke tailors and old-fashioned shaves with cut-throat razors.

START: Piccadilly Circus tube station.
FINISH: Green Park tube station.
LENGTH: 3.75 miles approx. Busy streets and parkland. Steps up into Waterloo Place.
REFRESHMENTS: Few facilities after Piccadilly. Café in St James's Park. Expect crowds around Buckingham Palace and St James's Park.

The Walk

Begin walking along the left-hand side of Piccadilly, a dual carriageway with a raised central section. Pass St James's church (which we will return to later in the walk) and arrive at ❶ **Hatchards**, the oldest bookshop in London, opened in 1797. A well-loved institution with a huge collection of books spread over five floors, Hatchards is also renowned for its celebrity book signings, comfortable atmosphere and staff who don't rush you.

Next door is another London institution, ❷ **Fortnum and Mason**, often cheekily dubbed 'the Queen's grocer', established in 1707 by William Fortnum, a footman to Queen Anne, and his landlord Hugh Mason. That original grocery store has grown into today's expansive emporium, recognised internationally for high quality goods and as an iconic symbol of Britain.

The firm's handsome neo-Georgian premises were built in 1926-7 and were extended along Piccadilly in a £24 million refurbishment in 2007. Fortnum and Mason has a celebrated tea shop and is famed for food hampers which can cost up to £1,000 – depending on the degree of luxury you're prepared to pay for.

Hatchards

Fortnum and Mason

Cross Piccadilly at the traffic lights and go through the arch of the imposing gatehouse of the ❸ **Royal Academy of Arts**, which is located in Burlington House, a rare example of a surviving grand mansion on Piccadilly. Originally built in the 1660s, it was remodelled in the Palladian style for the Earl of Burlington during 1715-17 and greatly enlarged in the 1860s when the RA and five other learned institutions moved in. The upper floor was refurbished in 1991 by Foster & Partners to create the airy Sackler Galleries.

Sir Joshua Reynolds' statue Reynolds (1723-92) was an influential portrait painter. With Thomas Gainsborough he established the RA and in 1768 was elected its first president.

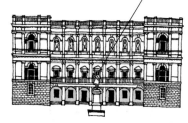

Burlington House

The famous summer exhibition of the Royal Academy has been held annually for over 200 years and comprises around 1,200 new works by both established and unknown artists chosen by an eminent jury.

The Royal Academy gatehouse

Burlington Arcade

Royal Arcade

Next door to the Royal Academy is the ❹ **Burlington Arcade**, best-known of Piccadilly's four 19th-century arcades of small shops selling traditional British luxuries. The Burlington was built for Lord Cavendish in 1819, reputedly to stop rubbish being thrown into his garden. To further the establishment of order, he recruited beadles (guards) from his own regiment to ensure that his wife and her friends could shop without being molested. Top-hatted and uniformed, beadles still patrol the arcade and have the authority to eject anyone who sings, whistles, runs or opens an umbrella. Modern shopping malls are not expected to follow suit.

Walk through the arcade, turn left and then left again into Old Bond Street, centre of London's fine art trade. Jewellers Cartier and Tiffany are over the road. Another arcade, the Royal, is at number 28.

Beyond the Ritz, Piccadilly opens out to the appropriately named Green Park, partly hidden by a large bus shelter. An M&S Simply Food store across the road is a good place to buy a snack to eat in the park.

Covering 47 acres, ❻ **Green Park** consists entirely of wooded meadows and, in contrast to its neighbouring parks, has no lake, no buildings and only a few monuments. It's just one part of the almost unbroken expanse of open land stretching for about two and a half miles from Whitehall to Notting Hill. The main avenue of trees slopes gently down to Buckingham Palace. To sit here eating your sandwiches while the sound of a military band taking part in the Changing of the Guard ceremony drifts gently up the hill is a rare treat.

Leave the park beside the ornate gates at the bottom of the hill, where the familiar sight of Buckingham Palace, one of London's most famous landmarks is revealed.

Ritz Hotel

Cross Piccadilly, turn right and pass the top end of St James's Street to the imposing ❺ **Ritz Hotel**.

Opened in 1906, the Ritz was the first steel-framed building in Britain and the first hotel in London to have en-suite rooms. Its design was modelled on the grand French hotels of the period, master-minded by the famed Swiss hotelier, César Ritz, who once managed the Savoy.

The opulence, service and luxury of the hotel caused a sensation in Victorian London and set the standards for future establishments – so much so that the word 'ritzy' has become a colloquialism for luxury.

Green Park

31

❼ **Buckingham Palace** is the official London residence of the British monarch and venue for state occasions and royal hospitality. It has also been a rallying point for the British people at times of national rejoicing and crisis.

Originally known as Buckingham House, the building which forms the core of today's palace was a large townhouse built for the Duke of Buckingham in 1705 on a site which had been in private ownership for at least 150 years. It was subsequently acquired by George III in 1761 as a private residence for Queen Charlotte and known as 'The Queen's House'.

The building was enlarged in the 19th century, principally by architects John Nash and Edward Blore, forming three wings around a central courtyard. It became the principal royal residence on the accession of Queen Victoria in 1837, although after the death of her husband Prince Albert in 1861, she preferred to live elsewhere.

The palace was bombed seven times during World War II with the most serious attack, in 1940, destroying the palace chapel. News film of the damage was shown in cinemas throughout the UK to show the common suffering of both rich and poor.

Union Flag Has flown over the palace since public outrage when there was no flag at half mast after the death of Diana, Princess of Wales in 1997. The Royal Standard is flown when the sovereign is in residence.

East front Added around 1900, including the famous balcony on which the Royal Family traditionally congregate to greet the crowds gathered outside on special occasions.

Queen Victoria Memorial Completed in 1911, sculpted by Sir Thomas Brock from 2,300 tons of white marble. Like the rest of The Mall, the memorial has a nautical theme. The subsidiary figures were a gift from the people of New Zealand.

The Mall Created as a ceremonial route as part of the development by Sir Aston Webb of a new façade for Buckingham Palace and the Victoria Memorial.

Buckingham Palace

Queen Anne's Gate

The Two Chairmen

Take Spur Road along the end of St James's Park and turn left along the right-hand side of Birdcage Walk, so called because there was a royal aviary here in the 17th century. Wellington Barracks are on your right, used by the various Guards regiments detailed to protect the royal residences. Looming over the Guards Chapel is the modern Ministry of Justice building, generally acknowledged to be one of the capital's great eyesores.

At the traffic lights beyond the chapel take a right turn along a walkway into **❽ Queen Anne's Gate**, architecturally one of London's finest streets.

The near-perfect early 18th-century terrace of beautiful houses has deep brown brickwork with white porches decorated with finely carved pineapples, foliage and god-like faces. A statue of Queen Anne stands in the street and her ghost is said to walk three times around the street on the night of 31st July, the anniversary of her death. Most of the houses are now occupied by government agencies.

The **❾ Two Chairmen** pub, at the end of St Anne's Gate, dates from 1683, and boasts original oak beams, period fireplaces, and a ban on 'modern intrusions' such as loud music or TVs.

The 'two chairmen', immortalised in the pub sign, refers to the two carriers of sedan chairs which could once be hired here. Pub signs originated in 1393 so that an inspector could identify the premises and check the quality of the ale.

Visit the Two Chairmen if you fancy some refreshment and a sit down but please note that, like many other city centre pubs, it has restricted opening at weekends when the area is quiet.

Walk around the double bend into Old Queen Street, another 17th-century architectural survivor. Turn left down Cockpit Steps, a narrow alleyway which once led to the royal cockfighting area.

Turn left back onto Birdcage Walk, return to the traffic lights where you entered Queen Anne's Gate, cross the road and go into St James's Park.

Whitehall from St James's Park

Old Queen Street

🔟 **St James's Park** extends to 58 acres and is the oldest of London's royal parks. In 1532, when the area was swampy marshland, Henry VIII acquired it for the Crown. James I ascended to the throne in 1603 and had the marsh drained so that he could keep exotic animals and birds. Influenced by his time in exile in France, Charles II had the park redesigned on his return. Further remodelling by John Nash in the 1820s created the park we see today.

Walk down the hill and onto the footbridge over the lake, where two extraordinary views are revealed. To the west Buckingham Palace peeks through the trees and to the east there's an almost fairy-tale view of the spires and domes of Whitehall Court and Horse Guards with the towers of the Foreign Office, seen across the willow trees of Duck Island.

The park is home to a myriad of ducks, geese and coots, while winding pathways and shrubbery all add to an agreeable, garden-like setting.

Cross the footbridge and take the pathway on your right which passes the park café. Continue up the slope to the Mall, the processional route from Trafalgar Square to Buckingham Palace.

The route, exactly 0.5 nautical miles (0.58 miles) long and perfectly straight, was designed by Aston Webb in 1906, together with a new façade for Buckingham Palace .

Cross the Mall to the broad flight of steps climbing to Waterloo Place. The steps divide ⓫ **Carlton House Terrace** into two equal sections 140m (460ft) long. The terrace, designed by John Nash, was built in 1827-33, one of his last grand designs before he died. There are nine houses in each section, all different, with other architects embellishing Nash's basic designs. Numbers 7-9 were the German Embassy until World war II, their interiors remodelled by Albert Speer, Hilter's favourite architect.

Best seen from the Mall, they are some of the most fabulously expensive properties in London. Number 18 was sold in 2013 for £250 million!

A house in Carlton House Terrace

Duke of York statue

A statue of the ⓬ **Duke of York** (1763-1827) stands where Carlton House was before the Prince Regent became bored with it and turned his attention to Buckingham Palace.

The 'Grand Old Duke of York' – of children's nursery rhyme fame – was the second son of George III, brother of the Prince Regent and Commander-in-Chief of the British Army at the time of the Battle of Waterloo (1815). His statue by Sir Richard Westmacott is set on an unusually tall column (38m/124ft) which wags of the time said was to avoid his creditors, as he died with £2 million debts (a huge sum at the time). Funds for the statue could only be raised by docking a day's pay from the entire British army.

Carlton House Terrace from the Mall

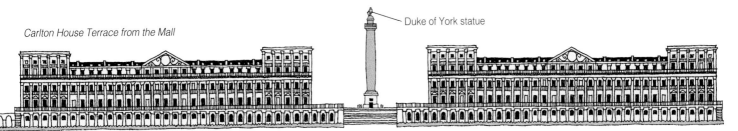

Duke of York statue

The Athenaeum

A statue of Edward VII stands at the centre of Waterloo Place, with those of lesser-known notables around the edges and in the neighbouring gardens.

Further on across Pall Mall and facing Waterloo Place is the **⑭ Guards Crimean War Memorial** which commemorates over 2,000 guardsmen who died in the Crimean War during 1854-56. It was sculpted by John Bell and erected in 1860. The three guardsmen figures were cast from the metal of Russian guns.

A figure of Honour, bearing wreaths in her outstretched arms surmounts the striking monument. It originally stood further down the square but was moved here to enable the statues of Florence Nightingale and Sidney Herbert (Secretary for War during the Crimean Campaign) to be added.

Beyond the Duke of York column is **⑬ Waterloo Place**, the culmination of Nash's grand plan, where Regent Street widens to a square, lined with neo-Classical buildings and notable for a fine collection of statues.

The Athenaeum, an elegant stuccoed block on the corner of Waterloo Place and Pall Mall, is one of London's most distinguished buildings. Built in 1827-30 , it was designed by Decimus Burton, a protegé of John Nash. Burton's father built many of Nash's designs. A fine Doric frieze runs along three sides of the building and above the entrance is a large gilt copy of the *Pallas Athena of Velletri* by E.H. Baily.

A raised kerbstone outside the gentleman's club has been there since 1830, installed to enable the Duke of Wellington to mount and dismount his horse when visiting.

The Guards Crimean War Memorial

Turn left around the Athenaeum into Pall Mall, which after the bright stucco of Waterloo Place can seen a little dull. Appropriately, some say, as this is a street mostly of gentlemen's clubs, those mysterious places where deals were done with decorum, and in comfort and privacy.

They developed from the coffee houses of the 19th century and are little changed since, apart that is from the opulent luxury often secreted behind their silent walls. However, for non-members the street still holds much of architectural interest.

The Travellers Club

Standing next to the Athenaeum is the **⑮ Travellers Club**, designed by Charles Barry and built 1829-32. It's one of the oldest of the Pall Mall clubs, established in 1819 so that gentlemen who travelled abroad could return hospitality to distinguished foreign visitors. Members are still required to have travelled abroad.

The **⑯ Reform Club** was founded by Edward Ellice MP, parliamentary whip for the Whig party. Originally a club for the political activists who brought about the Great Reform Bill of 1832, it no longer has a political stance and is purely a social club.

The Reform Club

The building, another neo-Classical Charles Barry design of 1842, is a two-storey palazzo in smooth Portland stone. It's also notable for being raised half a storey above street level and having its main rooms grouped around a glazed courtyard. In a major restoration in 2007 the building was cleaned and the old roof replaced with startling orange pantiles.

The club is forever associated with Jules Verne's *Around the World in Eighty Days* where the journey was conceived and the famous bet made. In 1981 it became first of the Pall Mall gentlemen's clubs to admit women.

The office building on the next corner looks surprisingly contemporary, built in 1956-8 to replace Sydney Smirke's Carlton Club (1847). Of white Portland stone and six storeys high, the Swedish modern style of the building became popular after the Second World War, when classical forms had become associated with totalitarianism.

100 Pall Mall

The Royal Automobile Club

Continuing along Pall Mall you come to the **⑰ Royal Automobile Club**, a private members club now unconnected with the motor services club, its former owners. Built during 1908-11, the club was designed in overblown French style by Mewès and Davis, who were also responsible for the Ritz Hotel.

The large-scale Portland stone façade conceals grand club rooms in Louis XIV style, three restaurants, two bars, a fully equipped business centre, a shop and a post office. Below ground there's Edwardian Turkish baths (renovated in 2003-4), several squash courts, a solarium and a spectacular Italian marble swimming pool.

The club boasts a membership of more than 11,000, so they must be doing something right.

The stand-out building in this part of Pall Mall is **⑱ Schomberg House** and not just because of its brown brick with red trim façade. It also has tall windows of Dutch proportions and decoration of French origin. The mansion was built around 1698 for the German Duke of Schomberg, a Huguenot general in the service of the British Crown.

The striking street frontage is all that survives of the original building, which had a rich and varied history. It was split into two and for a while three establishments which over time housed

Schomberg House

a quack doctor's surgery, a high-class brothel, a gambling den, a fashionable textile store, a picture dealer, an auctioneer, a haberdasher, a bookshop and offices of the War Office.

Thomas Gainsborough, the portrait painter, lived and worked in the building from 1774 until his death in 1788. The interior is now divided into modern open plan offices.

Edwin Lutyens designed the outside of the large building on the corner where Pall Mall widens into Marlborough Gate. Built in 1928, it currently incorporates a bank on the ground floor and flats above.

In possibly a light-hearted

The Lutyens' windows

moment, Lutyens designed the windows on each floor in different styles showing, 'how to get up a building without repeating yourself'.

The splendid Tudor gatehouse of
⑲ St James's Palace marks the end
of Pall Mall at the right-angle junction
with St James's Street.

The palace was built for Henry VIII
in 1536 on the site of a former leper
hospital. A fire in 1809 destroyed
much of it but the gatehouse survived
and restoration was quickly carried
out with the help of our old friend
John Nash. The palace was the
monarch's official London home from
1698 until Queen Victoria occupied
Buckingham Palace in 1837.

Prince Charles made it his base
until 2007, when he moved around
the corner to Clarence House where
the Queen Mother lived until her
death in 2002.

Berry Bros & Rudd

Handily positioned just across the
road from the palace is **⑳ Berry Bros
& Rudd**, supplier of wine to the royal
family since the reign of George III.
Other customers have included Pitt
the Younger, Lord Byron and the Aga
Khan.

Britain's oldest wine and spirit
merchant was established in 1698 at
the same St James's Street premises
as today. At the 'Sign of the Coffee
Mill', Berry not only supplied the
fashionable 18th-century 'Coffee
Houses' (later to become clubs such
as Boodle's and White's) but also
began weighing customers on giant
coffee scales.

The company now sells over 3,000
different wines and spirits worldwide,
stored in their vast cellars stretching
underground as far as Pall Mall.

St James's Palace

Continue up St James's Street where next door to Berry Bros & Rudd, and with an equally picturesque shop front, is another London institution, **㉑ James Lock & Co**, suppliers of 'Ladies' and Gentlemen's hats and caps'.

The company was founded in 1676 when Charles II was on the throne. The famous London bowler originated here and the company also made a hat with an eye shade for Lord Nelson and the plumed hat that the Duke of Wellington wore at Waterloo.

Continue uphill and take the first turning on your right along King Street. This takes you into **㉒ St James's Square** which, unusually for London is actually square. Laid out in 1665 it was the city's most regular planned square with individual houses of different designs and centrally placed streets. It has been a favourite of the aristocracy ever since, the north side being mostly intact with its original houses.

Chatham House (1734) Designed by Henry Flitcroft. Former home of the British Prime Minister, William Pitt the Elder. Now Royal Institute for International Affairs.

London Library A private lending library founded in 1845 by the historian Thomas Carlyle and others.

Lichfield House (1764-6), Designed by James Stuart with a balcony added around 1791.

The former Naval and Military Club, built 1726-8, Home of Lady Astor, an American socialite, who, in 1919, became the first woman to take a parliamentary seat in the House of Commons.

The former Libyan Embassy. Scene of the 1984 fatal shooting of policewoman Yvonne Fletcher, followed later in the year by the Libyan Embassy Siege.

William III statue by John Bacon, which has stood here since 1808.

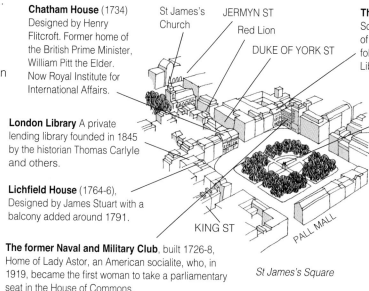

St James's Church   JERMYN ST   Red Lion   DUKE OF YORK ST   KING ST   PALL MALL

St James's Square

Leave St James's Square along Duke of York Street where there's a historic beer-house, The Red Lion, which survived the Blitz and has been here since 1788. It remains ostensibly unchanged since the early 1900s, and describes itself as a 'step back in time to an ornate Victorian gin palace'. Who can resist?

James Lock & Co

Lichfield House

From Duke of York Street turn left into **㉓ Jermyn Street**, with St James's Church on your right. Isaac Newton (1642-1727), discoverer of the Law of Gravity, lived at number 86, opposite the entrance to Prince's Arcade on the right. Jermyn Street is famous for classy shoe shops, bespoke shirts and men's outfitters. At the entrance to Piccadilly Arcade there's a statue of George 'Beau' Brummell (1778-1840), a dandy, close friend of the Prince Regent and the greatest 'celeb' of his day.

Pass behind Fortnum & Mason on the corner and turn right into St James's Street. White's Club is on your right.

St James's Church

㉔ St James's Church (1676-84) is one of Christopher Wren's best-known and most influential works. It was commissioned in 1972 as the parish church for the new district of St James's being developed by Henry Jermyn, Earl of St Albans.

Elegantly built of red brick with Portland stone dressings, it straddles the space between Jermyn St and Piccadilly, and was designed as a focal point for the view along Duke of York Street from St James's Square.

㉕ White's was established in 1693 by an Italian, Francesco Bianco, whose name translates to Francis White – hence White's. It moved to its current St James's Street abode in 1778.

White's is the original 'Old Boys' Club', the grandest, oldest and in some ways the weirdest. It has always attracted the establishment great and the good – and the not so good!

Drinking has always been part of the fabric and the club boasts a bar which 'has not shut for 200 years'. Members have been known to gamble on anything even, it's said, which raindrop will reach the bottom of the window first.

White's

White's is also notoriously difficult to gain entry to, and impossible if you're female. Only one woman, the Queen, has ever been allowed through the front door. Once, every Prime Minister, from Robert Walpole in the early 18th century to Robert Peel in the mid-19th, was a member, but David Cameron (a member for fifteen years) resigned in 2008 over the club's refusal to allow women members, despite his father, Ian Cameron, once being its chairman. The former Prime Minister is said to be the only member ever to have left of his own free will.

Walk to the top of St James's Street and turn left into Piccadilly. Continue past the Ritz Hotel to Green Park tube station, the end of this walk.

Soho

Places of interest

1 Palace Theatre
2 Coach & Horses
3 Three Greyhounds
4 Gay Hussar
5 Soho Square
6 St Patrick's Church
7 Hazlitt's Hotel
8 Ronnie Scott's
9 Bar Italia
10 French House
11 Quo Vadis
12 St Anne's Court
13 Blue Posts
14 Intrepid Fox
15 St Anne's Church
16 Queen's Theatre
17 Chinatown
18 Chinese dragons
19 Prince of Wales Theatre

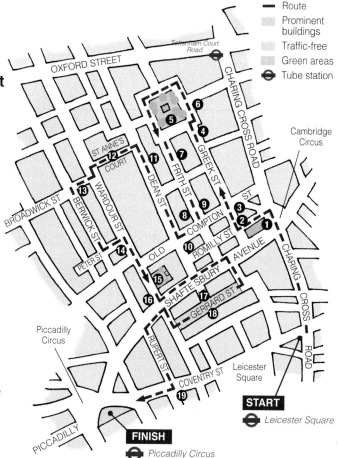

First developed in the late 17th century, Soho is famous for the pleasures of the table, the bottle and the flesh. During the 18th century it became one of London's most fashionable areas, but by the 20th century Soho had consolidated its reputation for bohemian entertainment.

The sleaze of the 1950s and 60s has largely disappeared but the narrow streets still attract a cosmopolitan mix of people to enjoy its many pleasures. Old Compton Street is the heart of the capital's gay community.

The architecture isn't spectacular but it's interesting and richly historic.

START: Leicester Square tube station.
FINISH: Piccadilly Circus tube station.
LENGTH: 2.25 miles approx. Narrow streets. Crowded, especially at night. Quietest in the morning. Soho doesn't wake up before lunchtime.
REFRESHMENTS: Restaurants, cafés, fast food outlets, bars and pubs. You shouldn't go hungry or dehydrate in Soho.

The Walk

Begin walking up Charing Cross Road, which still hangs onto a few of the bookshops it's famous for. The road crosses Shaftesbury Avenue at Cambridge Circus, where you can't miss the huge red-brick façade of the **❶ Palace Theatre**.

It was built in the 1880s by Richard D'Oyly Carte who hoped the theatre, one of London's largest, would become the home of English Grand Opera. That didn't happen and after a spell as a music hall it began to show films. Eventually, in 1925, the theatre became the venue for musicals, for which it's now well known. *Les Misérables* ran here from 1985 for a record-breaking nineteen years.

Andrew Lloyd Webber bought the building in 1983 and after a radical restoration in 2004 it was sold with some of his other houses to Nimax Theatres in 2012.

Cross to the northern side of the circus and walk down narrow Romilly Street, which runs between the theatre and the Spice of Life pub, to enter Soho itself.

Palace Theatre

The Cambridge

The Spice of Life pub. A Soho landmark and a leading live music venue. Past acts have included Bob Dylan, Cat Stevens, Paul Simon, the Sex Pistols and Jamie Cullen.

Prince Edward Theatre

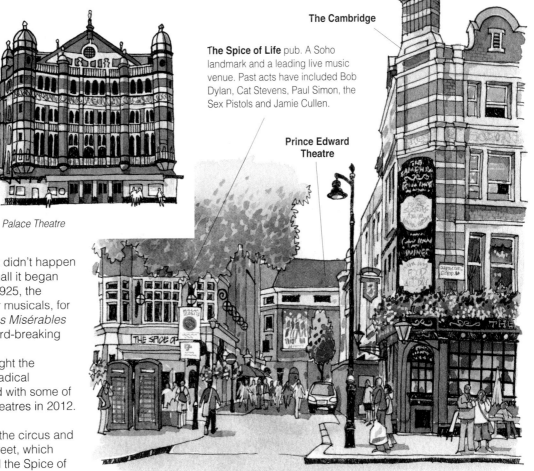

Cambridge Circus and the Moor Street entrance to Soho

43

Norman's Coach & Horses

The Gay Hussar

On the corner with Greek Street there's the **❷ Coach & Horses**, legendary haunt of Soho boozers such as the writers Keith Waterhouse and Jeffry Bernard. The sign outside calls it 'the West End's Best Known Pub' and it was also renowned for 'London's Rudest Landlord', Norman Balon, who ruled the place with the sharpest of tongues from 1943 until his retirement in 2006. It's now billed as 'Norman's Coach & Horses' in his honour. The satirical magazine, *Private Eye*, hosts fortnightly lunches in a hidden restaurant behind the bar and there are regular sing-songs around the 'ol' pianna'.

Further along and to your right on Old Compton Street, there's the **❸ Three Greyhounds**, an impressive half-timbered hostelry described as a 'traditional pub'. It got its name from the dogs used to hunt hares when Soho was open ground. Licensed premises have existed here since at least 1847 but the present building dates from the 1920s.

Continue walking north along Greek Street, named after the Greek church that stood in Hog Lane. Records show that Casanova stayed in this street in 1764.

Number 2 Greek Street was the **❹ Gay Hussar**, a celebrated Hungarian restaurant, opened in 1953, which became a favourite of left wing politicians. It's said to have been 'a socialist works canteen since Nye Bevan's day' in the 1940s.

After becoming a Soho institution the tiny restaurant finally closed its doors in 2018.

The Three Greyhounds

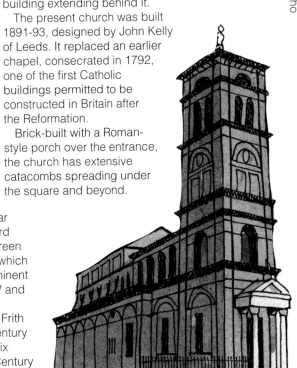

As you enter **❺ Soho Square** there's a large square building on your right with the words 'House of Charity' painted between the second and third storey windows.

The building dates to 1649 and was originally a private house. It later became local government offices, until 1862 when a charity bought it as a refuge for London's homeless. Now called 'The House of Barnabas', it runs an employment academy programme aimed at returning homeless people into work and independence.

Soho Square 'hut'

Soho Square was laid out in 1681 and enjoyed a brief period as the most fashionable address in London. But gradually it went out of favour and is now surrounded by a variety of rather bland buildings housing TV and film production companies and offices. The garden at the centre is pleasant enough, with its mock-Tudor hut a cheery Victorian addition.

The Farm Group HQ

Further round the square, near where Soho Street joins Oxford Street, there's an attractive green house, dating back to 1677, which is the headquarters of a prominent post-production facility for TV and films, the Farm Group.

As you exit the square into Frith Street you pass Twentieth Century House. Look up to the roof, six storeys high, where a '20th Century Fox' roundel can just be seen, which is unusually restrained for a Hollywood giant.

Soho Square is well-worth walking round – and looking up – especially where the great bell tower of **❻ St Patrick's Church** rears up through the garden's trees giving no indication of the huge building extending behind it.

The present church was built 1891-93, designed by John Kelly of Leeds. It replaced an earlier chapel, consecrated in 1792, one of the first Catholic buildings permitted to be constructed in Britain after the Reformation.

Brick-built with a Roman-style porch over the entrance, the church has extensive catacombs spreading under the square and beyond.

St Patrick's Church

Soon after you leave Soho Square you come to a Georgian style town house on your left. As engraved over the entrance, this is **❼ Hazlitt's Hotel**, built in 1718 and named after the essayist and critic, William Hazlitt (1778-1830), who died in this house and was buried in St Anne's churchyard.

The hotel is furnished as it was in Hazlitt's time but, as the Georgians rarely washed, now with plenty of modern bathrooms added.

Further down the street you can't miss **❽ Ronnie Scott's** famous jazz club, painted black with bright red lettering and oozing cool.

Scott played tenor saxophone, and founded the club with Pete King, a fellow saxophonist, in 1959. Since then most of the world's great jazz musicians have played here and it was the venue for Jimi Hendrix's final public performance in 1970.

Scott, also a world-class raconteur and wit, died in 1996. The club, under new management, had a makeover in 2006 and continues to attract top artists from around the world.

Hazlitt's Hotel

Ronnie Scott's jazz club

The upper floors of Bar italia

Opposite Ronnie Scott's and above **❾ Bar Italia** at 22 Frith Street, there used to be an attic workshop where in 1925 John Logie Baird (1888-1946) invented television. Jim Wallder, a grocer's delivery boy, became the first person to appear on television when Baird transmitted his image to a room next door.

Soho is generally a peaceful place these days, but during the 1950s and 60s the area was riddled with violent gang culture. Many of its leading exponents hung out in Bar Italia, then a trendy coffee bar, and huge fights would often erupt on the street outside.

When you reach Old Compton Street turn right and then right again into Dean Street. Pause at the corner and have a look left at at the **⑩ French House** (it's the one with all the French flags). Now a respectable bar and restaurant, it was originally a 19th-century gin parlour and latterly one of the favourite watering holes for many of London's Bohemian writers, actors, artists and musicians.

Maurice Chevalier and General de Gaulle also dined here, though probably not together.

The French House

Quo Vadis

Walk north along Dean Street. Just beyond the junction with Bateman Street is **⑪ Quo Vadis**, one of London's top-rated restaurants. It was founded in 1926 and has had a series of owners including the chef Marco Pierre White and the artist Damien Hirst. With a stack of awards, the restaurant now attracts a large clientele of glittering film, music and media celebrities.

Things were different between 1851 and 1856 when Karl Marx (1818-1883) and his family lived in two of the upper rooms. Three of his children died here during a cholera epidemic in 1854 and Marx described the accommodation as an 'old hovel'.

Two doors away, a blue plaque above the stage door of the Prince Edward Theatre claims that Mozart – then eight years old – 'lived, played and composed' in a house on this site during 1764-65.

St Anne's Court

Take the next turning on your left along **⑫ St Anne's Court**, now a pleasant walk-through, one of many that run between the main Soho streets.

During the 1960s, strip clubs lined these alleyways where in earlier times Jewish tailors would toil in the front windows. During the late 19th century there was a considerable Jewish community in this part of Soho, many of them refugees escaping persecution in Eastern Europe.

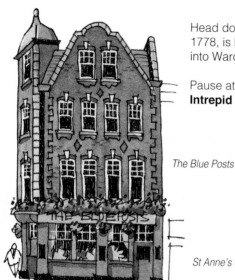

The Blue Posts

St Anne's Church

Head down Berwick Street where the famous market, dating from 1778, is held on weekdays. When you reach Peter Street turn left into Wardour Street.

Pause at the corner for a look at a stone plaque to ⑭ **The Intrepid Fox**. It's the only reminder of the live rock 'n' roll pub that used to shake this building, with the likes of Mick Jagger, Rod Stewart, the Sex Pistols and actor Richard Harris playing – and propping up the bar.

The Intrepid Fox was founded by Whig leader Charles James Fox in 1784, who promised free beer to anyone who gave him electoral support. The building was more recently threatened with demolition, but was eventually sold in 2006 and rocks on as a Byron burgerbar.

At the end of St Anne's Court cross Wardour Street into Broadwick Street opposite, then turn left into Berwick Street at the ⑬ **Blue Posts** pub.

There are three alehouses with that name in Soho and others elsewhere in London. They are thought to be early 'taxi' ranks, places where sedan chairs could be hired to transport drinkers home through the filthy streets.

Continue along Wardour Street to ⑮ **St Anne's Church**. The outer walls and 17th-century tower are all that survived the World War II bombing of 1940. The churchyard is raised some 8ft above street level due to around 60,000 bodies being buried here between 1695 and 1853. In 1891 it was laid out as a public garden, a beautiful, tranquil sanctury amid the bustle of modern Soho.

Queen's Theatre

With the **⑯ Queen's Theatre** on your right, turn left along busy Shaftesbury Avenue to the traffic lights near the Curzon Cinema. Cross over and walk down Gerrard Place into **⑰ Chinatown**.

London's Chinese population was originally concentrated around the East End docks at Limehouse but began to move into Soho during the 1950s. Chinatown now has more than 80 restaurants showcasing some of London's finest and most authentic Asian cuisine. Three ornate arches, build by Chinese artisans, straddle the pedestrianised streets.

Halfway along Gerrard Street you pass two fearsome **⑱ Chinese dragons**, carved in stone, which were donated by the People's Republic of China and unveiled by Prince Charles in February 2000 to celebrate the Chinese New Year.

Chinese dragons

Continue walking around the block and return via lower Wardour Street to Shaftesbury Avenue. The sweeping highway was cut though slums between 1877-86 and is named after the Earl of Shaftesbury (1801-85) in honour of his work to improve the living conditions of the poor.

With five theatres and two cinemas, Shaftesbury Avenue is now considered to be the centre of London's theatreland.

Turn left along the south side of the avenue, then opposite the Gielgud and Apollo theatres across the road, turn left down Rupert Street.

Gielgud Theatre

Chinese arch

The distinctive Art Deco tower of the **⑲ Prince of Wales Theatre** is straight ahead. Established in 1884 and rebuilt in 1937, it was refurbished by its current owner Cameron Macintosh in 2004. From showing French-style revues in the 1930s and variety shows featuring all the top British acts in the 1950s, the theatre now concentrates on blockbuster musicals.

Turn right, along Coventry Street into Piccadilly Circus, the end of your walk.

Prince of Wales Theatre

Whitehall & Westminster

Places of interest

1. Benjamin Franklin House
2. Ship & Shovell
3. Charing Cross station
4. Ministry of Defence
5. Banqueting House
6. Horse Guards
7. Horse Guards Parade
8. Dover House
9. Downing Street
10. The Cenotaph
11. Parliament Square
12. Westminster Abbey
13. St Margaret's Church
14. County Hall
15. Houses of Parliament
16. St John's, Smith Square
17. Millbank Tower
18. Tate Britain
19. MI6 Building
20. Vauxhall Bridge

— Route

Prominent buildings

Traffic-free

Green areas

Tube station

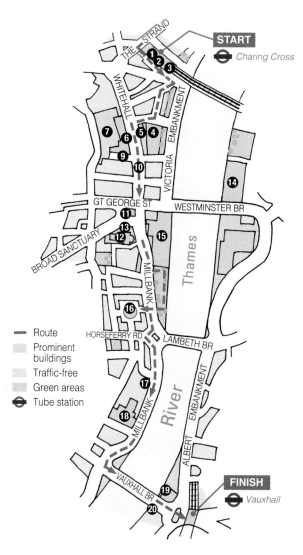

This area has been the centre of political and religious power in England for more than a thousand years. Kings built palaces and the great offices of state followed.

This walk visits majestic government buildings, iconic Parliament Square and the architectural masterpieces of Westminster Abbey and the Houses of Parliament.

There are also a multitude of statues of the famous and the not so well-known to puzzle over, and three bridges from which to enjoy river views.

Further along the Thames we'll take in a Baroque gem in Smith Square and the cultural treasure house of Tate Britain. There's also some oddities (some very odd) to enjoy along the way.

START: Charing Cross tube station.
FINISH: Vauxhall tube station.
LENGTH: 3.25 miles approx. Expect crowds in Whitehall and Parliament Square. Quieter in Millbank.
REFRESHMENTS: Surprisingly scarce for a top tourist area. Good restaurant at St John's, Smith Square and a Pizza Express on Millbank. Tate Britain has a restaurant and three cafés.

The Walk

Leave Charing Cross tube station and turn left along the Strand, then left again into the narrow pedestrianised part of Craven Street between the Next and Boots stores.

The alley soon opens to a handsome terrace of Georgian houses. ❶ **Benjamin Franklin's House** is at number 36. Built around 1730, it's the only remaining home of Benjamin Franklin (1709-90), the American-born polymath

Benjamin Franklin's House

who lived here for fifteen years. A key founder of the USA and the only statesman to sign all four documents that created the new nation, Franklin is also credited with being one of the people who discovered electricity. The house and museum are open to the public.

Further along Craven Street have a look along Craven Passage, the narrow street leading off left, where there's the ❷ **Ship and Shovell**, an unusual, possibly unique, Victorian pub. Oddly, it consists of two separate buildings on either side of the street which are connected underground by a shared cellar. You can see double without even going through the door!

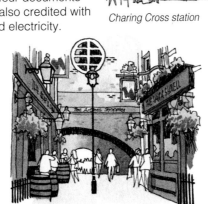
The Ship & Shovell

Player's Theatre

Taxi Driver's Hut Established in 1875 as a resting place for horse-drawn Hansom cab drivers. Still a few left around the city.

Charing Cross station

Continue to the bottom of the street where it widens into Victoria Embankment. The Thames is straight ahead with Hungerford Bridge on your left which carries trains serving the south-east of England. The walkways on either side of the bridge were completed in 2003.

The original ❸ **Charing Cross station** was built on the site of the old Hungerford Market in 1864. In 1990, most of the area above the platforms was covered by Embankment Place, a huge, Post-Modern style office and shopping complex, rising nine storeys above the railway tracks.

The Ministry of Defence & Banqueting House

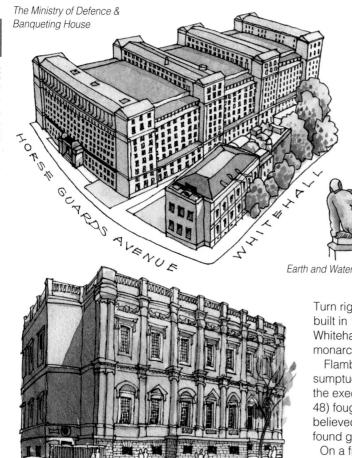

Earth and Water

Banqueting House

Cross into Whitehall Place. To your left is the Gothic tower of the former Liberal Club, part of a block of luxury residential apartments built in 1884 and modelled on a French chateau.

Take the first left into Whitehall Court where the great bulk of the **❹ Ministry of Defence** building fills the view ahead. This huge neo-Classical edifice of eight storeys was built between 1938-59, designed by Vincent Harris to house the Air Ministry and the Board of Trade. The northern entrance is flanked by two monumental statues, Earth and Water by Charles Wheeler. The ministry's defence competence was brought into question in 1991 when the Provisional IRA launched a mortar shell at Downing Street from a van parked in this street. It exploded in the back garden of Number 10, blowing out some windows while Prime Minister John Major was holding a Cabinet meeting.

Turn right along Horse Guards Avenue to the **❺ Banqueting House**, built in 1622 by Inigo Jones, one of the few surviving parts of the huge Whitehall Palace which was the main London residence of English monarchs from 1530 until it burnt down in 1698.

Flamboyant banquets were held in the upper storey under a sumptuous painted ceiling by Rubens, but it's most famous as the site of the execution of Charles I. After defeat in the English Civil War (1642-48) fought between Royalist and Parliamentary forces, the king, who believed in the divine right of kings to have absolute rule, was tried and found guilty of treason.

On a freezing day in January 1649 he stepped from one of the upper windows of Banqueting House onto a scaffold erected in Whitehall, and was beheaded by a single stroke of the executioner's axe.

Horse Guards

Cross Whitehall at the traffic lights to **❻ Horse Guards,** a large Palladian style building finished in 1758 to a design by William Kent, which became the headquarters of two major Army commands: the London District and the Household Cavalry. Two troopers on black horses in little stone houses guard the building. Two others on foot pose for tourist photographs in the courtyard.

Go into the yard and through the archway into **❼ Horse Guards Parade**, once the Palace of Whitehall's tiltyard or jousting field where tournaments were held for the amusement of Henry VIII.

With the garden of Downing Street to the south and the elegant Admiralty building to the north the parade ground now forms an impressive setting for pageantry occasions. Trooping the Colour, when marching foot soldiers and military bands parade their flags to the monarch, is held here every June.

Return through the archway to Whitehall and turn right, heading for the distant Houses of Parliament.

An equestrian statue of Earl Haig, Commander-in-Chief of the British forces during World War One, stands in the centre of the road. Unveiled in 1937, the installation of the statue by Alfred Frank Hardiman was thought to be as controversial as Haig's tactics were during the war.

❽ Dover House, opposite the statue, was built as a private house in 1758. It was designed by the prolific Palladian architect James Paine with Henry Holland transforming the façade in 1787. The result has been described as some of Whitehall's finest architecture.

Further along there's a striking memorial to The Women of World War II, a bronze sculpture by John Mills, unveiled in 2005, which commemorates women's war work by depicting the uniforms they wore hanging on pegs.

Dover House

Crowds on the pavement nearby will identify the gated and guarded entrance to **❾ Downing Street,** built in the 1680s by Sir George Downing, on the site of a mansion called Hampden House. The Prime Minister, the Chancellor of the Exchequer and the Chief Whip all have official residences and offices along the short street. For security reasons, iron gates were erected at the Whitehall end in 1989 and public access was ended.

The famous black door of Number 10, the official residence of the Prime Minister, opens only from the inside. There are actually two doors, which are exchanged when one needs repainting. Originally black oak, they're now made of blast-proof steel and require eight men to lift each one. The zero of the number '10' is set at a slight angle on the door as a nod to the original number which had a badly-fixed zero.

The doorway of Number 10 Downing Street

Number 10 contains some 100 rooms. After 300 years of London pollution the external brickwork became blackened; the bricks are actually a yellow colour but are now painted black to keep their familiar appearance.

The Cenotaph

❿ The Cenotaph, principal war memorial of Britain, stands in the centre of Whitehall near Downing Street. It commemorates those who died in the two world wars and all the wars that British troops have fought since.

The simple and dignified memorial was designed by Sir Edwin Lutyens and unveiled in 1920. The annual Remembrance Sunday ceremony is held here in November when the sovereign, politicians and veterans all lay wreaths to remember the fallen.

Downing Street

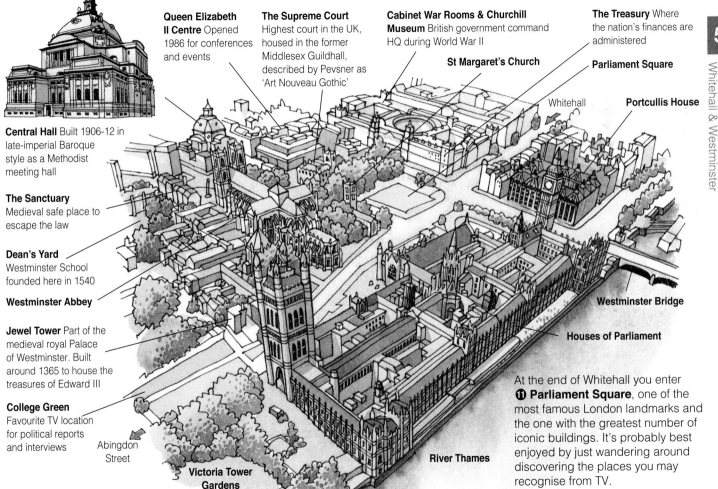

Central Hall Built 1906-12 in late-imperial Baroque style as a Methodist meeting hall

The Sanctuary Medieval safe place to escape the law

Dean's Yard Westminster School founded here in 1540

Westminster Abbey

Jewel Tower Part of the medieval royal Palace of Westminster. Built around 1365 to house the treasures of Edward III

College Green Favourite TV location for political reports and interviews

Abingdon Street

Victoria Tower Gardens

Queen Elizabeth II Centre Opened 1986 for conferences and events

The Supreme Court Highest court in the UK, housed in the former Middlesex Guildhall, described by Pevsner as 'Art Nouveau Gothic'

Cabinet War Rooms & Churchill Museum British government command HQ during World War II

St Margaret's Church

The Treasury Where the nation's finances are administered

Parliament Square

Portcullis House

Whitehall

Westminster Bridge

Houses of Parliament

River Thames

At the end of Whitehall you enter
⓫ Parliament Square, one of the most famous London landmarks and the one with the greatest number of iconic buildings. It's probably best enjoyed by just wandering around discovering the places you may recognise from TV.

One of the most famous façades in the world, the twin towers at the western end of ⑫ **Westminster Abbey** command attention, but the beautifully decorated Lady Chapel at the eastern end is equally striking. The Abbey stretches some 162m (530ft) from end to end. Mainly Gothic in design, it's the traditional venue for coronations and the burial site for British royalty and national heroes.

An abbey has stood on this site since 620. Edward the Confessor began his own 'minster' here, which was dedicated in 1065, only ten days before Edward himself was interred in the foundations. William the Conquerer was crowned in the Abbey in 1066 setting a precedent for almost every British monarch since. Completed in 1259, the Chapter House has the finest medieval tiled floor in England. The first 'Mother of Parliaments' met here from 1257, the origins of the modern House of Commons.

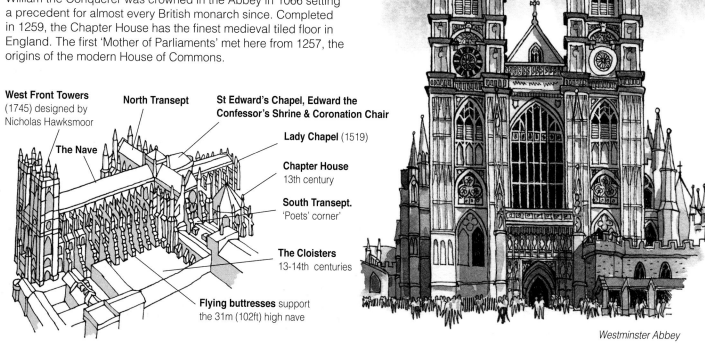

West Front Towers (1745) designed by Nicholas Hawksmoor

North Transept

St Edward's Chapel, Edward the Confessor's Shrine & Coronation Chair

The Nave

Lady Chapel (1519)

Chapter House 13th century

South Transept. 'Poets' corner'

The Cloisters 13-14th centuries

Flying buttresses support the 31m (102ft) high nave

Westminster Abbey

The simple Anglican **⓭ Church of St Margaret** stands in the shadow of Westminster Abbey. Originally founded in the 12th century by Benedictine monks, it became the parish church of the Palace of Westminster in 1614, when the Puritans, unhappy with the highly liturgical Abbey, chose to hold Parliamentary services in the more 'suitable' St Margaret's; a practice that has continued ever since.

Sir Walter Raleigh, famous for potatoes and tobacco, and the poet John Milton are buried here. St Margaret's is also a popular venue for society weddings. Samuel Pepys and Sir Winston Churchill were married here.

London Eye The tallest Ferris wheel in Europe, opened in 2000. It carries 32 sealed and air-conditioned egg-shaped passenger capsules, each representing one of the London Boroughs. Each capsule holds 25 people who are free to walk around, though seating is provided. One revolution takes about 30 minutes and the views across London are sensational.

The view across the Thames from Victoria Embankment

St Margaret's Church

A walk over Westminster Bridge is recommended for the famous view of the full length of the Houses of Parliament across the river. A bridge was first built here in 1750, the first crossing of the Thames since the medieval London Bridge. The present bridge, opened in 1862, was designed to complement the Palace of Westminster, being painted the same green as the benches in the House of Commons.

A huge stone lion stands on the bridge beside County Hall. A riverside feature since 1837, it used to stand by Hungerford Bridge at the entry to the Lion Brewery. It was moved here in 1966 when the brewery was demolished.

The main six-storey part of **⓮ County Hall**, designed by Ralph Knott in an Edwardian Baroque style, was opened in 1922 by King George V. Other parts of the building were added in the 1930s and 1970s. After serving as the headquarters of Greater London Council for 64 years until it was abolished in 1986, County Hall now houses visitor attractions and offices.

Victoria Tower
98m (323ft) high. Houses three million documents of the Parliamentary Archives in almost six miles of steel shelves spread over 12 floors.

Lords Chamber The lavishly decorated debating area measures 14m x 25m (46ft x 80ft). The benches in the Chamber are coloured red. The upper part of the Chamber is decorated by stained glass windows and by six allegorical frescoes representing religion, chivalry and law.

Central Tower
Octagonal in shape and 92m (300ft) tall, stands above the Central Lobby. It's part of the building's ventilation system or as cynics have it, for the removal of hot air.

Commons Chamber
Opened in 1950 after the Victorian chamber had been destroyed in a 1941 air raid during World War II. The Chamber measures 14m x 21m (46ft x 68ft) and the benches are coloured green.

Clock Tower Commonly known as Big Ben is 97m (316 ft) high. Weighing 13 tons, the largest of the five bells in the belfry (the actual 'Big Ben') strikes the hours. It has a crack which gives a distinctive sound, first heard across London in 1859.

Portcullis House MPs offices opened in 2001 at a cost of £235 million. Westminster tube station was rebuilt at the same time underneath.

Westminster Bridge

The Terrace One of the most exclusive dining places in London

The Houses of Parliament

The Palace of Westminster has been the seat of the two houses of the United Kingdom parliament since 1512. The Old Palace, a medieval building, was mostly destroyed by fire in 1834. Its replacement, a gothic masterpiece by Charles Barry and Augustus Pugin, who both died during its thirty-year construction, was completed in 1870.

The palace has over 1,100 rooms, 100 staircases and 3 miles of passages spread over four floors. The ground floor is offices, dining rooms and bars, with the first floor housing the main rooms of the palace, including debating chambers, lobbies and libraries. The building is currently undergoing an extensive restoration programme estimated to cost £5.7bn over 35 years. Both houses of parliament are expected to relocate elsewhere for possibly 15 years.

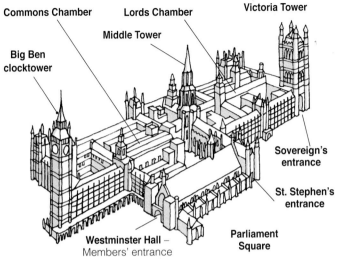

Commons Chamber

Lords Chamber

Victoria Tower

Middle Tower

Big Ben clocktower

Sovereign's entrance

St. Stephen's entrance

Westminster Hall –
Members' entrance

Parliament Square

Westminster Hall is the oldest surviving part of the original Palace of Westminster, built for William II in 1097. It has the widest clearspan medieval roof in England, measuring 21m across by 73m long (68ft x 240ft). Charles I, Sir Thomas More and Guy Fawkes were all condemned to death at trials in this hall. It's now mainly used for ceremonial occasions.

Leave Parliament Square along Abingdon Street and just beyond the Victoria Tower turn left into the gardens for a look at *The Burghers of Calais,* a much-admired cast of Auguste Rodin's original in Paris. Continue along the riverside, then turn right at the ornate Buxton Memorial Fountain and take the path out of the gardens into Millbank. Cross the road at the crossing and continue along Dean Stanley Street into Smith Square.

The square is dominated by **⑯ St John's**, considered to be the finest example of English Baroque architecture anywhere. It was built in the reign of Queen Anne during 1714-28, to a Greek-cross plan with enormous Doric columns marking the north and south entrances. Four chunky corner towers are topped by stone pineapples.

Bombed and severly damaged in 1941, the church was restored by Marshall Sisson in 1965-69 and reopened as a concert hall. The reasonably-priced Footstool Restaurant in the crypt is open for weekday lunches and on concert evenings.

The rest of the square is worth exploring with some pleasing 18th-century houses built at the same time as the church.

St John's, Smith Square

Return to Millbank, cross the road and walk along the riverside to Lambeth Bridge. In 1860 there was a suspension bridge crossing here. The current structure with five steel arches opened in 1932. Obelisks at both ends of the bridge are topped by stone pinecones, ancient symbols of hospitality.

Continue past the ⓱ **Millbank Towe**r, built in 1963 when glass towers first became popular. However, this one looks rather lonely and out of place. Originally built for the Vickers Armstrong group, it was headquarters of the British Labour party between 1995 and 2000.

Close by is ⓲ **Tate Britain**, built in 1897 on the site of the old Millbank Prison, used between 1816 and 1890 as a massive holding facility for prisoners awaiting transportation to Australia.

The original building, commissioned by the sugar magnate Sir Henry Tate to a design by Sidney R.J. Smith opened in 1897 and has been greatly remodelled and extended since.

Tate Britain displays a huge collection of British art from the 16th century to the present day, including the priceless J.M.W. Turner bequest of 300 paintings and some 20,000 watercolours and drawings.

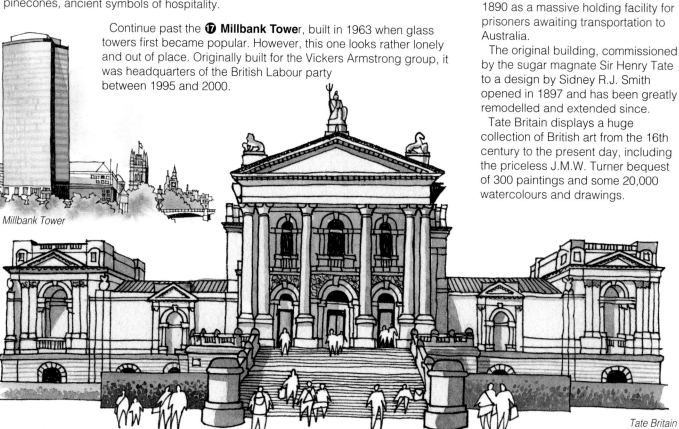

Millbank Tower

Tate Britain

The MI6 building

Across the river stands the distinctive **⑲ MI6 building**, headquarters of the British Secret Intelligence Service since 1994. It was designed by Terry Farrell & Co after winning a competition to develop the site. Resembling an Art-Deco stepped tower, the building is much ridiculed and has been called Legoland, Babylon-on-Thames, the Vauxhall Trollop – and worse.

Certainly it's built as a fortress, bristling with security cameras inside and out, bomb and bulletproof walls, triple-glazed glass blocking electronic eavesdropping and jamming, extra-stout doors – and two moats!

Much of the construction is below ground to protect sensitive areas such as the computer control room from potential terrorist attack. There are also rumours of a secret tunnel from here to Whitehall.

Flamboyant and ostentatious, this isn't the kind of building you can keep secret, but thankfully the only significant attacks on it so far have been in James Bond films.

Cross **⑳ Vauxhall Bridge**, which is surprisingly wide, (25m/82ft), with five steel arches. Opened in 1906, it replaced a cast iron bridge that had stood here since 1816. The piers of the bridge are decorated with huge statues of the Arts & Sciences by F.W. Pomeroy and Alfred Drury.

Vauxhall Bridge

As you cross the bridge a strange-looking structure is revealed on the far side. Two tracks point skywards like the launch pad for a massive vehicle to pounce on the MI6 building.

Closer, it's revealed as the switchback roof of the Vauxhall bus station. Designed by Arup Associates, the two cantilevered arms contain 167 solar panels, which provide a third of the bus station's electricity. Adventurous architecture it may be and creditably green but the shiny structure looks completely out of place here. Also does it actually keep the rain off waiting bus queues?

However, like it or loathe it, the roof does provide a lively talking point at the end of our walk.

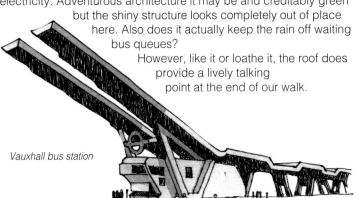

Vauxhall bus station

WALK 6

Chelsea

Places of interest

1. Sloane Square
2. Royal Court Theatre
3. Peter Jones
4. John Sandoe Books
5. Cheltenham Terrace
6. Saatchi Gallery
7. Royal Hospital Chelsea
8. National Army Museum
9. Tite Street
10. The Red House
11. Chelsea Embankment
12. Peace Pagoda
13. Physic Garden
14. Swan House
15. Cheyne Walk
16. Boy with a Dolphin
17. Albert Bridge
18. Cheyne Walk Brasserie
19. Thomas Carlyle's House
20. West House
21. King's Road
22. Wellington Square

Rich and famous, Chelsea is the embodiment of success and good living in fine houses. From a riverside village it developed into a fashionable bohemian district and is now the haunt of bankers, film stars and media moguls.

It's a fascinating area to walk round, and away from the King's Road is surprisingly quiet and peaceful. Apart from Wren's magnificent Royal Hospital, the architecture is on a domestic, residential scale, albeit an extremely wealthy one. This circular walk will take you to some of the most interesting.

START & FINISH: Sloane Square tube station.
LENGTH: 2.5 miles approx. No steep hills or steps.
REFRESHMENTS: King's Road. Cafés at the Royal Hospital and National Army Museum. Fine dining at Cheyne Walk Brasserie.

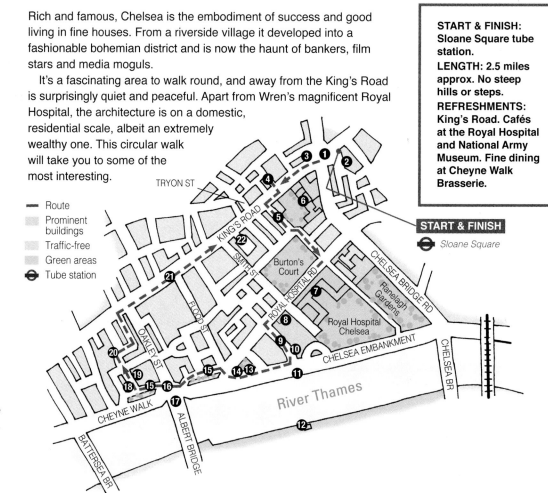

- Route
- Prominent buildings
- Traffic-free
- Green areas
- Tube station

START & FINISH
Sloane Square

Sloane Square

THE WALK

Exit Sloane Square station into **❶ Sloane Square**, which is actually long and rectangular. It's surrounded by mainly nondescript commercial buildings and has a hard-surfaced centre aisle, softened by plane trees. The square is a busy shopping area and road junction with traffic converging from Knightsbridge, the King's Road and Pimlico. It was laid out in 1780 and named after Sir Hans Sloane the weathly physician and collector who bought the manor of Chelsea in 1712.

To your right is the redbrick **❷ Royal Court Theatre**, opened in 1888, designed by the well-respected theatre architect, Walter Emden. Now home to the English Stage Company, it has a long history of fostering radical new drama.

Royal Court Theatre

Head along the left-hand side of the square to **❸ Peter Jones Department Store**, more a way of life to wealthy Chelsea residents than a mere shop. Construction on the building began in 1936 but stalled during the war. Designed by William Crabtree with various consultants, its use of curtain walling on the façade is considered to be one of the finest examples in London. A £100 million renovation in 2004 brought the interior of the store stylishly up-to-date. For a building designed in 1936, it still looks strikingly modern.

You are now into the King's Road, high street of modern Chelsea and one of the most fashionable shopping areas outside the West End.

Peter Jones

John Sandoe Books

Pass the Duke of York Square and the entrance to the Saatchi Gallery. Opposite a grassy playing field you can cross the King's Road to narrow Blacklands Terrace for a visit to ❹ **John Sandoe Books**.

The veteran Chelsea bookseller died in 2007 but sold the independent bookshop to members of staff in 1989. Once a grooming parlour for poodles, this much-loved old-fashioned shop is a cornucopia of 25,000 books, groaning shelves and narrow steps, and counts Elton John and Tom Stoppard amongst its many celebrity customers.

Return across the road and go into ❺ **Cheltenham Terrace**. Beyond the huge 1930s Whitelands House flats complex there's a line of elegant Georgian houses which enjoy a fine view of the ❻ **Saatchi Gallery** across a school playing field.

The building was completed in 1801, designed by John Sanders who was also responsible for the Royal Military Academy Sandhurst. It was originally the Royal Military Asylum and was a school for the children of soldiers' widows. In 1892 it was renamed the Duke of York's Royal Military School.

Cheltenham Terrace

The school eventually moved to new premises and the Asylum building was taken over by the Territorial Army in 1911 and renamed the Duke of York's Barracks.

It was sold in 2000 to Cadogan Estates and after extensive redevelopment, including the creation of the Duke of York Square, the building was let for a variety of uses.

The Saatchi Gallery relocated here in 2008. Led by Charles Saatchi, the former advertising mogul, the gallery promotes a wide spectrum of contemporary art and has had a profound influence on popular British culture, bolstered by a history of critical extremes and vibrant media controversy.

The Saatchi Gallery from Cheltenham Terrace

Royal Hospital Chelsea

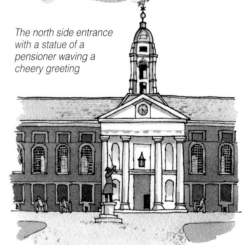

The north side entrance with a statue of a pensioner waving a cheery greeting

Continue into Franklin's Row with the ❼ **Royal Hospital** in sight ahead. To your right is Burton's Court, a private sport and leisure ground owned by the hospital and used to raise funds for its running costs and maintenance.

King Charles II commissioned the elegant buildings of the Royal Hospital from Christopher Wren in 1682 as a retirement and nursing home for British soldiers. The hospital cares for some 400 pensioners, including women since 2009, who receive board and lodging, a uniform and nursing care. They are affectionately known as 'Chelsea pensioners'.

The extensive grounds are open to the public, along with some of the buildings, and since 1913 have been the venue for the Royal Horticultural Society's world-famous Chelsea Flower Show.

Public access is through the London Gate entrance onto East Road. The first turn left takes you to the Margaret Thatcher Infirmary. The coffee shop is located to the right of the main entrance.

With the Royal Hospital on your left, head down Royal Hospital Road where substantial red brick houses line the right hand side.

Pass the recently redeveloped **8** **National Army Museum** which tells the stories of British forces around the world in permanent and special exhibitions.

At the functional St Winifred's Convent on the corner, turn left into **9** **Tite Street**, centre of Chelsea's radical artistic and literary community of the late 19th century.

The playwright and aesthete Oscar Wilde lived at number 64, painters John Singer Sargent and the American James McNeill Whistler lived at number 31, while Augustus John had a studio at number 33. Chelsea property prices were not like they are today and studio flats with soaring windows were affordable then – even for bohemian artists.

Numbers 44-46 Tite Street

Edward Godwin, one of the leading architects of the day, built numbers 44-46 Tite Street in Queen Anne style in 1878-9. Number 46 is known as the Tower House due to its soaring eight-storey height.

Godwin designed many houses for Chelsea's emerging avant-garde artistic community including the controversial White House for James McNeill Whistler. The house had to be sold after Whistler lost an expensive court case against the art critic, John Ruskin, and was demolished in 1968.

Further along Tite Street there's a more contemporary contribution to Chelsea's architectural art scene, the **10** **Red House**, designed by Tony Fratton Architects in 2001. Severe and plain with red French limestone cladding and bronze window frames, it's been described as having, 'something of the look of a monumental gravestone'. The building's façade does have a mysterious air about it, which cleverly conceals a sumptuous interior.

The Red House

Tite Street takes you to the ⓫ **Chelsea Embankment**, completed in 1874 to a design by Joseph Bazalgette, as part of the Metropolitan Board of Works grand scheme to provide London with a modern sewage system.

The development swept away much of old Chelsea, leaving many of the more romantic residents mourning the loss of the boatyards and alehouses along the waterfront.

Swan House

The Peace Pagoda

The river is quieter now and the view across to Battersea Park much changed, as a golden Buddha now gazes serenely back from the opposite riverbank.

In 1985, on the fortieth anniversary of the dropping of the atomic bomb on Hiroshima, the Nipponzan Myohoji Buddhist Order donated the 35m (100ft) high ⓬ **Peace Pagoda** to the park, one of more than 80 that have been built around the world. Permission to build the peace pagoda was the last legislative act of the Greater London Council before it was abolished.

A right turn onto the right-hand side of the Embankment takes you past the ⓭ **Chelsea Physic Garden**, founded 1673. It's an idyllic place in summer and a reminder of when Chelsea was a village surrounded by orchards and farms. The botanical garden, London's first, was expanded by Sir Hans Sloane in 1712. Its closeness to the river creates a micro-climate that enables exotic plants to thrive.

Standing next door to the Physic Garden is the magnificent ⓮ **Swan House**, built in 1875-6 by the architect Richard Norman Shaw. Architecturally it's a mixture of the Queen Anne and Arts & Crafts movements, said to be 'the finest Queen Anne Revival building in London'.

The four-storey, red-brick house has a vast ballroom, a cinema and a basement pool. It also seats 20 in its dining room and has parking for five cars. After a ten-year restoration the house was put on sale in 2007 for £32 million.

Cheyne Walk houses and gardens

Over the years, Cheyne Walk has attracted a galaxy of celebrity residents, including the 19th century writer George Eliot, the poet Swinburne and artist Dante Gabriel Rossetti, the British prime minister David Lloyd George and writer Vera Brittain during World War II, plus Mick Jagger, Keith Richards, Marianne Faithfull and footballer George Best in the 'swinging sixties'.

At the junction with Oakley Street there's a striking statue, ⑯ *Boy with a Dolphin* by David Wynne, erected here in 1975. Wynne used his youngest son, Ronald, then aged 10, as a model. Ronald died in 1999 when he was just 35 and the sculpture is now his memorial. The apparently gravity-defying appearance of the boy is achieved with the use of a double cantilever. Two other casts of the statue are in America.

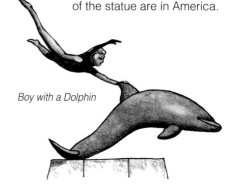

Boy with a Dolphin

Cross the end of Royal Hospital Road into ⑮ **Cheyne Walk** which, when Chelsea was a sleepy village outside London, was a quiet riverside walkway lined with fine houses and trees overlooking the Thames. After the Chelsea Embankment was created, the river was diverted away from the houses, narrowing it at this point. The Embankment is now usually busy with traffic but the houses, set back on their own side road behind front gardens, retain much of their previous serenity.

 Cheyne Walk is one of London's most sought-after addresses with its rich (in every sense) mix of 18th-century townhouses and an abundance of period gems.

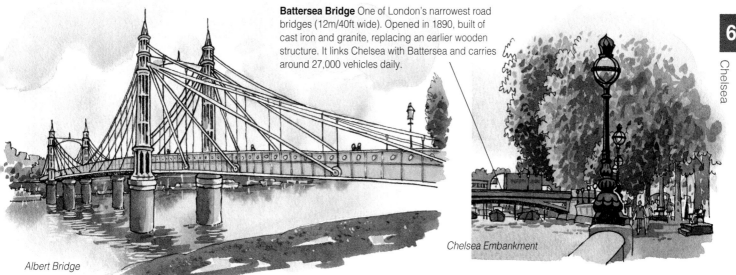

Battersea Bridge One of London's narrowest road bridges (12m/40ft wide). Opened in 1890, built of cast iron and granite, replacing an earlier wooden structure. It links Chelsea with Battersea and carries around 27,000 vehicles daily.

Albert Bridge

Chelsea Embankment

The toll booths on Albert Bridge

The first part of Cheyne Walk rejoins the Embankment where the **⑰ Albert Bridge** crosses the Thames to Battersea. Though pretty in pink, the bridge has never quite made it as a bridge. Designed and built by Rowland Mason Ordish in 1873, it soon proved to be structurally unsound and despite a number of redesigns and with a roadway only 8.2m (27ft) wide it's unable to cope with modern traffic. Even marching troops from Chelsea Barracks have to break step while crossing.

It was also commercially unsuccessful as a toll bridge. Six years after opening, the bridge was taken into public ownership and the tolls lifted. The toll booths remain in place and are the only surviving examples of bridge toll booths in London. In 1992, the bridge was rewired and painted in an unusual colour scheme designed to make it more conspicuous in poor visibility and less vulnerable to damage from shipping.

However, despite its shortcomings as a bridge, when it's illuminated by 4,000 bulbs at night, the Albert Bridge is one of West London's most striking landmarks.

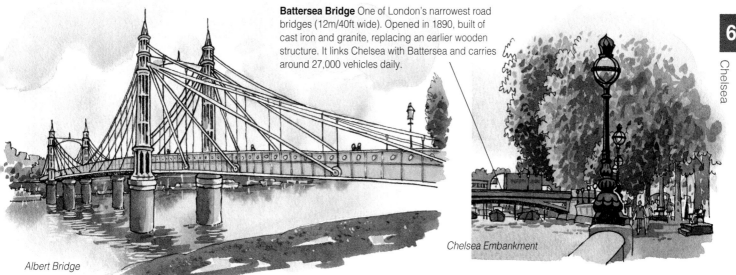

Number 38 Cheyne Walk

Continue along Cheyne Walk on the western side of Oakley Street. Number 38 was built in 1904 as a studio house for the artist C.L. Christran. The studio is on the top two floors behind the gable with the porthole window and was designed by one of the leading architects of the 1900s, Charles Robert Ashbee. He was one of the leading lights of the Arts & Crafts movement, as can be seen from the street railings of black ironwork with ornamental gold balls.

At the junction with Cheyne Row you arrive at the **18** **Cheyne Walk Brasserie**, once a Victorian pub and now a chic and modern French-style eating house. An open grill has pride of place in the Belle Epoque dining room where gourmet dishes are prepared. As you'd expect in this upmarket part of London, it's not cheap to enjoy the brasserie's Provençal-style cooking, but neither is it prohibitively expensive.

Thomas Carlyle's House

Cheyne Walk Brasserie

Turn right into Cheyne Row, a delightful sloping terrace of brown-stone houses overhung by trees. Number 24 is **19** **Thomas Carlyle's House**, an elegant Queen Anne-style house, dating from 1708, where the Scottish historian and philosopher, and his wife Jane, also a writer, moved to in 1834.

They were the literary celebrity couple of the day and helped turn Chelsea into an artistic mecca with many of the literary giants of the time visiting them here. Jane died in 1866 and Carlyle died in the drawing room of the house in 1881.

Now owned by the National Trust, the house is open to the public and kept much as it was when the Carlyles lived here. They paid rent of only £35 a year, a pittance compared to today's ultra expensive Chelsea property.

West House

Continue on Glebe Place, passing the end of Bramerton Street and yet more of Chelsea's desirable houses. Stay on the twisting road to eventually join the King's Road opposite William Yeoward's store, appropriately a designer of luxury interiors and accessories. Turn left along the King's Road for less than a mile back to Sloane Square and the end of this walk.

The **㉑ King's Road** was until 1830 a private road for King Charles II to travel to Kew. It's traditionally associated with 1960s style and the punk generation. Most of the counterculture has now been gentrified and with its street cafés, familiar chain store names and low rise buildings, the King's Road these days isn't much different from the High Street of any prosperous English town. Provided, of course, you ignore the grand squares and streets leading off it.

Pass the Roman Catholic church on the corner and carry straight on into Glebe Place, heading for the prominent red house at the top of the slope.

㉒ West House, designed by Philip Webb for the artist George Price Boyce, has been described by Historic England as 'one of the earliest examples of the Queen Anne Revival style and one of the landmarks of 19th-century British architecture'.

Various artists lived in the house after Boyce's death and in 2011 it was bought by a French businessman for £20 million.

Wellington Square

Tryon Street off the King's Road

㉒ Wellington Square, one of a number of fashionable squares off the King's Road, was completed in 1852, coinciding with the death of the Duke of Wellington, hero of Waterloo. His body was brought to Chelsea Hospital for lying in state, inspiring the square's name. The author of Winnie the Pooh, A.A. Milne, lived in the square and it's said to be the fictitious home of James Bond.

Knightsbridge & Kensington

Places of interest

1 Harrods
2 Brompton Oratory
3 V&A Museum
4 Natural History Museum
5 Science Museum
6 Royal College of Music
7 Royal Albert Hall
8 Albert Memorial
9 Flower Walk
10 Royal Garden Hotel
11 Kensington Palace
12 Serpentine Gallery
13 Serpentine Sackler Gallery
14 Reformers' Tree
15 Speakers' Corner
16 Marble Arch

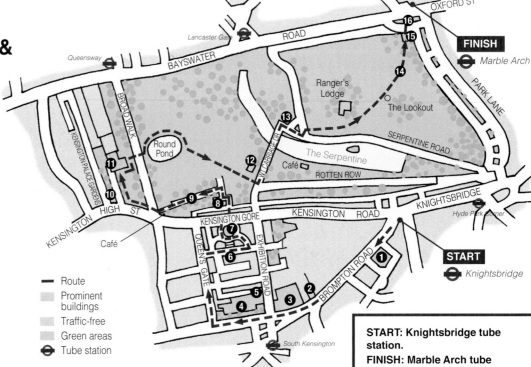

— Route
▨ Prominent buildings
▨ Traffic-free
▨ Green areas
☻ Tube station

This is an ultra-expensive residential area, home to many of the world's richest people and British royalty. The walk starts at Knightbridge's signature stores Harvey Nichols and Harrods and takes in Britain's largest collection of museums. From the iconic Royal Albert Hall we go on to visit Kensington Palace, from where the tour takes on a rural aspect with a stroll across Hyde Park, ending at Marble Arch.

START: Knightsbridge tube station.
FINISH: Marble Arch tube station.
LENGTH: 2.5 miles approx. No hills or steps.
REFRESHMENTS: Cromwell Road museums, Hyde Park cafés and galleries.

Harrods

Cross Brompton Road to ❷ **Brompton Oratory**, main centre of Roman Catholic worship in London before Westminster Cathedral was built in 1903. Consecrated in 1884 and built to a design by Herbert Gribble, the large Oratory building is faced in Portland stone, with the vaults and dome in concrete. The dome was heightened in profile and the cupola added in 1895, so it now stands 61m (200ft) tall. The London Oratory is one of the custodians of classic Catholic liturgy with mass being celebrated daily in Latin.

Continue walking along this side of the street, swinging right along the broad dual carriageway of Thurloe Place, which leads to Cromwell Gardens and Cromwell Road.

THE WALK

Exit Knightsbridge tube station across the road from Harvey Nichols. Turn left into Brompton Road where the great bulk of ❶ **Harrods** department store soon hoves into view. With its green and gold canopies, gold-braided commissionaires, thronging tourists by day and lit up like a luxury cruise ship at night, Harrods is symbolic of the area itself.

Wholesale grocer Charles Henry Harrod established his Knightsbridge shop in 1849. After a fire in 1883, the founder's son, Digby Harrod, built the present landmark building with its distinctive dome housing a water tank filled by the company's private water supply.

Harrods is now the world's largest store, occupying a five acre site with over a million square feet of retail space and some 330 departments.

Brompton Oratory

This part of South Kensington is generally called the museum district, which began with the 1851 Great Exhibition in Hyde Park. After its success, museums, colleges, schools and the cultural centre of the Albert Hall were founded, many in grandiose buildings, potent symbols of Victorian confidence.

The V&A Brompton Road entrance

The ❸ **Victoria and Albert Museum** (usually abbreviated to V&A) has grown gradually and greatly since its beginnings in 1852 when it was housed in a utilitarian iron-framed building. The famous Cromwell Road façade, added by Aston Webb during 1899-1909, is decorated with 32 sculptures of English artists and craftsmen.

The V&A is the world's largest museum of decorative arts and design, housing a permanent collection of over 4.5 million objects ranging from early Christian devotional objects to cutting-edge furniture design. The collection spans 5,000 years from ancient times to the present day in virtually every medium.

Spread over six levels and with 150 different galleries you would have to walk more than seven miles to visit them all.

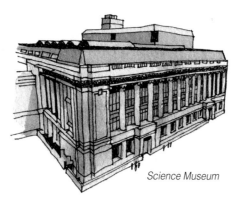

Science Museum

Natural History Museum

The ❹ **Natural History Museum** is a treasure-trove of life and earth sciences, housing some 70 million items within five main collections: Botany, Entomology, Mineralogy, Palaeontology and Zoology, including specimens collected by Charles Darwin. Opened in 1881, the vast cathedral-like building is a masterwork in itself, designed by Alfred Waterhouse in his own idiosyncratic Romanesque style.

Rather hidden-away in Exhibition Road behind the Natural History Museum is the ❺ **Science Museum**, the third of Cromwell Road's trio of treasure houses. The museum boasts a massive collection of more than 300,000 exhibits, from steam engines to space craft, computers to medicine and robots to flying machines.

Royal College of Music

Continue along Prince Consort Road to the imposing Royal School of Mines by Aston Webb, who also designed the V&A. Monumental sculptures around the entrance are Victorian melodramas rendered in stone.

Across the road is Kensington Gore, a canyon of red-brick mansion blocks that funnels you to the **❼ Royal Albert Hall** without having to climb any steps.

The glass and iron-domed landmark was completed in 1870 by engineers Fowke and Scott. Elliptical in shape and approximately 225m (735ft) in circumference, the hall was originally designed to hold 8,000 people. A great mosaic frieze, depicting '*The Triumph of Arts and Sciences*', runs around the outside. Since its opening by Queen Victoria, the world's leading artists from every genre have appeared here.

Great Exhibition and Prince Albert memorial by Joseph Durham (1863). Moved here in 1899. 13m (42ft) high in granite and Portland stone**.**

If you can tear yourself away from the attractions of the museums turn right into Queen's Gate, a tree-lined boulevard, wide enough for a central parking reservation. Grand stucco terraces built during the 1850s line one side, the majority converted into vast flats, hotels and embassies. Various academic buildings fill the right-hand side.

Turn right into Prince Consort Road, where red brick begins to dominate. The **❻ Royal College of Music** on your right was founded by Royal Charter in 1882. The College's impressive building was designed by Sir Arthur Blomfield in Flemish Mannerist style and built in 1892-94.

Opposite is the unmistakable Royal Albert Hall. A broad flight of stone steps leads to a statue of Prince Albert, honouring the part he played in planning and organising the Great Exhibition of 1851.

Royal Albert Hall from Prince Consort Road

Work your way around the hall to the Royal College of Organists, built in 1857, a four-storey, highly decorated building in cream, maroon and pale blue. Oddly, a frieze across the front depicting musicians contains no organist.

Next door and fronting onto Kensington Gore is the Royal College of Art, built 1962-73, which boasts David Hockney among its long list of eminent alumni.

Cross Kensington Gore at the traffic lights and enter Hyde Park with the awesome Albert Memorial to your left.

The ❽ **Albert Memorial** was commissioned by Queen Victoria in memory of her beloved husband, Prince Albert, who died of typhoid in 1861. Designed by Sir George Gilbert Scott in an extravagant Gothic Revival style, the monument was opened in 1872 by the Queen.

Matching her grief, the memorial is on a massive scale, 54m (176ft) tall and took over ten years to complete, at a cost of £120,000 (about £10 million today) met by public subscription.

The centrepiece is a gold figure of Prince Albert seated beneath a canopy, said to be inspired by a medieval town cross, and decorated with multi-coloured marble, stones, mosaics, enamels, wrought iron and some 200 sculpted figures. Restrained, it isn't.

Albert Memorial

Gated entrance to the Flower Walk

Take the pathway heading away from the memorial and turn left into the ❾ **Flower Walk**, a lovely avenue of of trees and flowerbeds.

The largest of London's Royal Parks, Hyde Park covers 275 acres. Combined with adjoining Kensington Gardens it makes up 625 acres of open parkland – bigger than Monaco – in the centre of the most populous city in Europe.

Originally, it was the private hunting ground of Henry VIII, land seized at the Dissolution of the Monasteries in 1536. James I made it public space in 1637 and since then the park has been the venue for duels, horse racing, highwaymen, demonstrations, rock concerts, parades and much more.

Royal Garden Hotel

The Flower Walk ends at a small outdoor café. Continue on the pathway straight ahead where you will soon see the five-star ❿ **Royal Garden Hotel** through the trees. Occupying an enviable location overlooking Kensington Gardens and Hyde Park, the hotel was built in 1965 on the site of an earlier one which dated back to 1800.

Designed by Richard Seifert, the building has had its share of criticism both for its appearance and location. It certainly looks out of place amongst Kensington's grand Victorian villas and stately royal apartments, and Princess Margaret is said to have been upset because it was on her doorstep. With the gateway to Kensington Palace actually adjoining the hotel, maybe she had a point.

Just before you reach the end of the park turn right onto Dial Walk which takes you to the famous golden gates of ⓫ **Kensington Palace** where acres of flowers were left after the death of Diana, Princess of Wales in 1997. She had an apartment here from 1981 until she died.

The palace was developed from an earlier mansion by Christopher Wren and others in the late 17th century. King William and Queen Mary wanted the conversion done quickly, so it was built of brick rather than stone. They moved in during 1689 and continued to rebuild, adding a gallery, the Queen's Apartments and a new entrance.

Queen Victoria was born in the palace and lived here until 1837, when she became queen. Half of it is open to the public, the rest is private apartments for members of the royal family and their staff.

Kensington Palace

William III statue

A flamboyant statue of William III in front of the palace, sculpted by Heinrich Karl Bauke, was a gift of Kaiser Wilhelm, a German relative of Edward VII. It's thought that the swaggering figure was the inspiration for Captain Hook in J.M. Barrie's *Peter Pan*.

The pathway on your right takes you around to the east side of the palace where there's a more respectful sculpture, that of a regal Queen Victoria sculpted by Princess Louise, the sixth of the queen's nine children.

Head east around the Round Pond, created in 1730 by George II. It isn't actually round and, covering seven acres, is more an ornamental lake than a pond. Beyond the pond you'll find a pathway heading east to the distant Serpentine Gallery.

Serpentine Gallery

The **⑫ Serpentine Gallery** houses temporary exhibitions of major contemporary artists' work, transforming its space to suit the exhibits, sometimes even spilling out into the park.

Take West Carriage Drive which crosses the park from Kensington Gore in the south to Bayswater Road in the north. Walk over Serpentine Bridge, the boundary with Kensington Gardens, built in the 1820s as part of a redevelopment by Decimus Burton, a contemporary of John Nash. The narrow and twisting Serpentine was created in 1730 when Caroline, the queen of George II, dammed the Westbourne River forming a relatively shallow lake with a maximum depth of 12m (40ft). Boating and swimming events are held on the water.

The Great Exhibition of 1851 was held here with the Serpentine as its centrepiece. Joseph Paxton designed the Crystal Palace, a large exhibition hall, which was later moved to a site on Sydenham Hill where it was destroyed by fire in 1936. Exhibits from the exhibition and its success inspired the creation of the museums visited earlier.

Beyond the bridge you come to the **⑬ Serpentine Sackler Gallery** located in a former 1805 gunpowder store. Designed by Pritzker Architecture Prize laureate Zaha Hadid, the gallery opened in 2013 and presents world-renowned exhibitions of art, architecture and design throughout the year.

Serpentine Sackler Gallery

Cross West Carriage Drive to the car park on Serpentine Road and join a walkway across the park, passing the Rangers Lodge and the Lookout, an unusual venue for events.

Serpentine Bridge

Marble Arch

Eventually, you arrive at the meeting point of nine pathways marked by a beautiful ground mosaic, the ⓮ **Reformers' Tree**. Created in black and white pebbles by Harry Gray in 2000, it commemorates the struggle for political enfranchisement in the 19th century.

When the historical tree was burnt down during the Reform League riots in 1866, the remaining stump became a notice board for political demonstration and a gathering point for Reform League meetings. In 1872, the Commissioner of Works designated a spot about 150 yards away for these gatherings – Speakers' Corner.

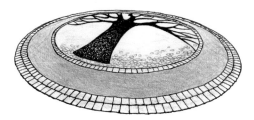

The Reformers' Tree

Continue on the pathway straight ahead to ⓯ **Speakers' Corner**, the London venue for open-air speaking, debate and discussion. Speakers can talk on any subject, providing the police consider it to be lawful. Prosecutions are rare but virulent hecklers and the heavy hand of modern political correctness have reduced the entertainment value for casual onlookers.

Cross Cumberland Gate at the northern end of Park Lane, one of the capital's classiest addresses and a valuable acquisition on a UK Monopoly board. However, Park Lane's appeal as a residential location was severely impaired during the 1960s, when the road, which runs for around three quarters of a mile between Hyde Park Corner and Marble Arch, was turned into a noisy, three-lane highway. Despite that, Park Lane remains well upmarket, with a number of five-star hotels and – appropriately – several sports car showrooms.

Across an open square ahead you'll see the ⓰ **Marble Arch**, which John Nash designed in 1827 as the entrance to Buckingham Palace. Too narrow for the grandest of coaches to pass through, the arch was installed here in 1851 as a corner piece for Hyde Park, close to the site of the old Tyburn gallows where public hangings were held in front of baying crowds until 1783.

This is the end of the walk and after the relative tranquility of Hyde Park the crowds may come as a shock. Happily they are unlikely to be baying.

WALK 8

Bloomsbury

Places of interest

❶ Bedford Square
❷ British Museum
❸ Russell Square
❹ Senate House
❺ Hotel Russell
❻ The Brunswick Centre
❼ Mary Ward Settlement
❽ Tavistock Square
❾ British Medical Association
❿ Woburn Walk
⓫ St Pancras Parish Church
⓬ Euston Station
⓭ Fire Station
⓮ Unison HQ
⓯ British Library
⓰ St Pancras Renaissance London
⓱ Midland Grand Hotel
⓲ King's Cross station

- ▬▬ Route
- Prominent buildings
- Traffic-free
- Green areas
- 🚇 Tube station

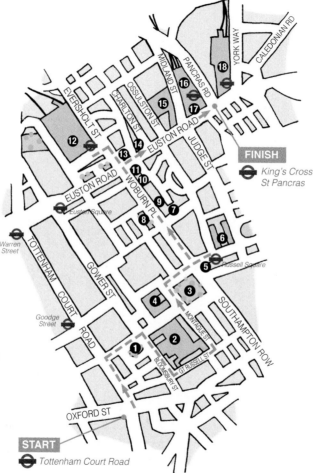

Bloomsbury has long been associated with literature, art and learning. It began as a fashionable residential district laid out between the late 17th and early 19th centuries, mainly by the Dukes of Bedford. Several writers of the Bloomsbury Group lived in the area during the early 1900s. These days it's a mix of academia and offices rather than residential.

The architecture is an interesting mix of little gems and the spectacular. Included in this walk are three squares, the British Museum, the British Library and three famous rail stations, all different in design and character.

START: Tottenham Court Road tube station.
FINISH: King's Cross St Pancras tube station.
LENGTH: 2.25 miles approx, along generally busy streets. No hills or steps.
REFRESHMENTS: Russell Square, The Brunswick, British Library and all rail stations.

THE WALK

From the tube station walk down the right-hand side of busy Tottenham Court Road. At the Jack Horner pub turn right, along Bayley Street into tranquil ❶ **Bedford Square**.

Built 1775-83 as the showpiece for the Bedford Estate, the square is one of the best preserved set pieces of Georgian architecture in London. It was the second square to be built on the Bedford estate after Bloomsbury Square a century earlier. Plain four-storey houses in brick with ornamental Coade stone line all four sides. At the centre, an oval-shaped garden filled with mature London plane trees is for the exclusive use of residents. In keeping with the area's literary heritage, most of the houses were occupied by publishers until the 1980s, but many have now been turned into offices. Fortunately, the façades and beautiful doorways are unaltered.

Numbers 32-39 house the Architectural Association, a leading architecture school founded in 1847. Some of the houses bear blue plaques recording famous residents. Two on number 35 commemorate 19th-century doctors: Thomas Wakley, who founded Britain's leading medical journal, the Lancet, and Thomas Hodgkin who worked to help persecuted Jews and the London poor.

Bedford Square. A good place to sit and put the world to rights.

Leave the square at its eastern corner and walk along Bloomsbury Street, turning first left into Great Russell Street and the majestic British Museum.

Bedford Square doorways

British Museum

Despite its name, Great Russell Street is quite narrow, but pleasantly overhung by trees outside Bloomsbury's greatest treasure, the ❷ **British Museum**. The world's oldest public museum, it was established in 1753 to house the collection of the physician Sir Hans Sloane. Since then it has grown to more than seven million objects, originating from all continents, which illustrate and document the story of human culture from its beginnings to the present.

   The 1847 façade facing Great Russell Street is a characteristic building of Sir Robert Smirke, with 44 Ionic columns 14m (46ft) high, closely based on the ancient temples of Greece. Architecturally, the building was hauled into the 21st century with the addition in 2000 of Sir Norman

Foster's inspired Great Court with the famous old reading room at its centre. The area, much praised for both design and construction, is the largest covered space in Europe and has a lightweight roof of 3,312 glass panels, each of a different size.

Continue along Great Russell Street beyond the museum and turn left into Montague Street, an avenue of Georgian houses, most converted into small hotels or flats. This brings you to ❸ **Russell Square**, another part of the extensive Bedford Estate, laid out on the 5th Duke's gardens by James Burton, a property developer and contemporary of John Nash.

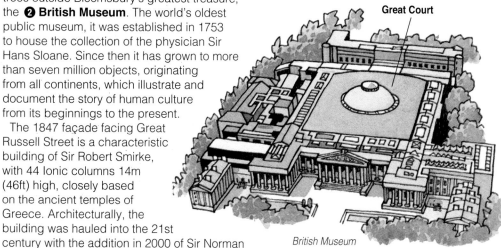

Great Court

British Museum

Senate House

The University of London occupies much of this district with the Art Deco ❹ **Senate House**, the University of London's administrative centre, commanding the western side of Russell Square. Built in 1932-37 and 690m (210ft) high with 19 floors, it was designed by Charles Holden, who was also responsible for a number of London tube stations. During World War II the building was used by the Ministry of Information and is thought to be the inspiration for the Ministry of Truth in George Orwell's novel *1984*.

Originally, Russell Square contained large terraced houses occupied mainly by upper middle class families. A number survive along the southern and western sides, with the end of Lasdun's 1979 Institution of Education building prominent on the northern edge.

In 2002, the square was re-landscaped, returning the garden at the centre to its original early 19th century layout by Humphry Repton, with a modern fountain added.

Hotel Russell/ The Principal London

Russell Square Gardens

One of the capital's most flamboyant hotels, the ❺ **Hotel Russell** was the first large incursion into Georgian Bloomsbury. Built in 1898 and twice as high as its then domestic neighbours, it was designed by Charles Fitzroy Doll, based on a French chateau near Paris. Clad in brick with decorative terracotta the hotel has colonnaded balconies and prancing cherubs beneath the main columns. Life-sized statues of four British queens adorn the the main entrance and the lobby is of multicoloured marble.

After a lengthy refurbishment, the Russell was reopened in 2017 as a five-star luxury hotel and rebranded as 'The Principal London'.

The Brunswick Centre

Leave Russell Square at the northeast corner and take a short detour along Bernard Street for a look at ❻ **The Brunswick Centre**, built in 1965-73, controversially designed as an antidote to high-rise towers for social housing.

Two parallel stepped blocks of flats face each other like stadium terracing across a raised internal plaza, edged by shops and cafés, with a cinema and an underground car park.

After a £22 million refurbishment in 2006, which included painting the grey concrete complex cream, the centre was rebranded as 'The Brunswick'.

Return to Woburn Place, a broad and busy highway, and turn right, heading for Tavistock Square, but just before reaching it, take a short diversion right to the ❼ **Mary Ward Settlement** in Tavistock Place. Built in 1895-8 to a

design by Smith & Brewer, the building is considered to be one of the best examples of an Arts and Crafts building in London.

Mary Ward was a Victorian novelist who founded an adult education centre which moved to Queen Square, Bloomsbury in 1982. The building is now a conference, events and exhibition centre.

Mary Ward Settlement

Retrace your steps and enter ❽ **Tavistock Square**, designed by Thomas Cubitt in 1806-26. A terrace of his houses survives along the west side. The public garden at the centre has a meditative statue of the Indian pacifist protester Mahatma Gandhi, sculpted by Fredda Brilliant and installed in 1968.

There's also a bust of Bloomsbury author and former resident, Virginia Woolf.

The standout building in the square is the ❾ **British Medical Association Headquarters**, begun by Edwin Lutyens in 1911-13 but halted during World War II. The grand brick Tavistock façade was completed by Wontner Smith in 1922-9.

Gandhi statue

One of London's four suicide bombings on the 7th July 2007 occured outside the building when a bomb was detonated on a bus. A memorial to the 13 victims is located in the gardens.

British Medical Association Headquarters

Before you reach the end of Woburn Place look out for **⑩ Woburn Walk**, a narrow alley on your right which opens to a restored street of bow-fronted shops designed by Thomas Cubitt in 1822. They're well worth the short detour.

St Pancras Parish Church & the Caryatids

Set on the corner with Euston Road, **⑪ St Pancras Parish Church** dates to 1819-22, designed by H.W. and W. Inwood. It's regarded as one of the earliest and finest Greek Revival churches in London. Similar to Gibb's St Martin-in-the-Fields, an octagonal bell tower stands above a giant six-column Ionic portico.

The church's most unusual features are two tribunes with entablatures supported by caryatids flanking the apse at the east end. Each terracotta caryatid holds a symbolic extinguished torch or an empty jug reflecting their position above the burial vault. They were designed by John Charles Felix Rossi but clearly based on the classical Acropolis of Athens.

Set on one of London's busiest roads the Portland stone of the building has been stained with pollution which has resisted most attempts to clean it .

Fire Station

The **⑬ Fire Station** on the corner of Eversholt street was designed by W.E. Riley of the LCC Architects Department in 1901-2. The red brickwork and Portland stone are typical of the English 'Arts and Crafts' Free Style which originated in domestic designs. This is one of the first examples of it used in a public building.

Cross at the lights to the **⑫ Euston Station** side of the street.The station building is set back from the street across a narrow park and hidden by trees. A good thing say many critics as, despite an impressive width of some 197m (646 ft), the building, opened in 1968, is in dull functional style. The main facing material is polished dark stone, complemented by white tiles, exposed concrete and plain glazing. The station is dark and gloomy – both inside and out.

A statue by Marochetti of Robert Stephenson stands outside the station. He was best known as a bridge engineer but also worked with his father, George, in the construction of railways.

Euston Station

Head down the left-hand side of Euston Road away from the station. You will soon come to the pristine white headquarters of **⓮ Unison**, one of Britain's largest trade unions with more than 1.3 million members.

It was built during 2008-11 to a modernist design by Squire and Partners. The listed building of the Elizabeth Garrett Anderson Hospital, built in 1898 next door, had to be included in the design and has been converted into offices and meeting rooms.

Continue along Euston Road to the conclusion of this walk, a collection of buildings each of significant cultural, historical and architectural importance: The British Library, the Midland Grand Hotel plus St Pancras and King's Cross stations.

Unison headquarters

Originally part of the British Museum, the commission to build larger premises for the **⓯ British Library** was awarded to Sir Leslie Martin, architect of the Royal Festival Hall, in 1962. Finding a suitable site took ten years and the actual construction another twenty. The library, which provides storage for 12 million books and space for 1,176 readers, finally opened in 1997. With architecture both immense and extraordinary, it has been hailed as the finest public space created in the late 20th century.

The library holds a multitude of treasures including the Magna Carta and many other important manuscripts and historical items. The interior is universally praised for its space, light, delivery of books, restaurants and coffee shops, which, like the library, are open to casual visitors. Enjoy.

Barlow's train shed

Great Northern Hotel

St Pancras International

King's Cross

Midland Grand Hotel
now the St Pancras
Renaissance London Hotel

British Library

EUSTON ROAD

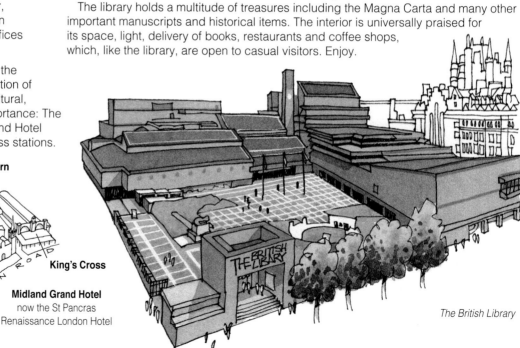

The British Library

After a £800 million restoration incorporating the Eurostar train terminus in 2007 and the addition of shops, bars, cafés and restaurants ⑯ **St Pancras station** has itself become a destination rather than just somewhere to pass through.

Henry Barlow built the still impressive roof of the engine shed in 1863-7, using the then new material of wrought iron. It was a triumph both of design and construction, a gigantic parabolic vault 30m (98ft) high with a span of 75m (246ft), at the time the largest in the world.

George Gilbert Scott, architect of the Midland Grand Hotel, built 1865-71, which forms the station's façade, regarded Barlow's creation as the work of a mere engineer and set about constructing his own Victorian masterpiece, an ornate concoction of English, Italian and Flemish Gothic, with a large central tower. Opened in 1876 it was one of the most sumptuous hotels of its time.

After a period of decline it closed in 1935, was threatened by demolition and used as office space. When Eurostar came to the station, the hotel was revitalised, being lavishly restored and extended at a cost of £200 million. It reopened in 2011 with the equally grand new name of ⑰ **St Pancras Renaissance London Hotel.**

St Pancras Renaissance London Hotel and the British Library from Euston Road

⑱ **King's Cross** is the terminus of the East Coast main line, opened in 1850 to accommodate the massive influx of visitors to the Great Exhibition. Designed by railway engineers Lewis and Joseph Cubitt in 1852, the station is memorable for its massive brick façade with two arches marking the roofs of the train sheds. Each spans 26m (85ft), separated by a central clocktower 37m (120ft) high.

A major renovation began in 2007 with the Western Concourse opened in 2012 and the original Victorian entrance restored and opened in 2014. New underground ticket halls and escalators with more than 300 metres of passageways now makes changing lines and services much easier.

King's Cross

The walk ends here with a choice of two mainline stations and numerous tube lines available.

The South Bank & Covent Garden

Places of interest

1. London Eye
2. Shell Centre
3. Hungerford Bridge
4. Royal Festival Hall
5. Queen Elizabeth Hall
6. National Theatre
7. Waterloo Bridge
8. Somerset House
9. One Aldwych
10. Savoy Hotel
11. Covent Garden
12. London Transport Museum
13. St Paul's Church
14. Royal Opera House
15. Bow Street Magistrates Court
16. Theatre Royal Drury Lane
17. One Kemble Street
18. Bush House
19. King's College London
20. St Mary-Le-Strand

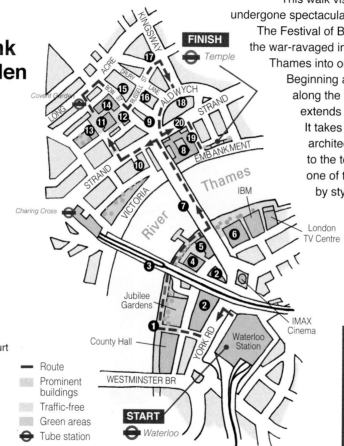

Route
Prominent buildings
Traffic-free
Green areas
Tube station

FINISH — Temple

START — Waterloo

This walk visits three London landmarks that have undergone spectacular conversions from their original uses. The Festival of Britain in 1951 sparked development of the war-ravaged industrial area on the south bank of the Thames into one of London's major cultural districts. Beginning at the London Eye, the walk continues along the popular Thameside promenade which extends between Vauxhall and Tower Bridges. It takes you past radical – and controversial – architecture before crossing Waterloo Bridge to the tourist mecca of Covent Garden, set in one of the city's earliest squares, surrounded by stylish Georgian and Victorian buildings. Pass the Royal Opera House and the Theatre Royal in Drury Lane before visiting elegant Somerset House, built as 18th-century government offices and now a much-admired public arts and cultural centre.

START: Waterloo tube station.
FINISH: Temple tube station.
LENGTH: 2.5 miles approx, along busy streets and the riverside promenade. Gentle slopes. Steps up to Waterloo Bridge.
REFRESHMENTS: Plenty of cafés and restaurants throughout.

THE WALK

Leave Waterloo tube station and follow the signs for South Bank and ❶ **The London Eye**. It's only close-up at the riverside that the massive construction of the ferris wheel can be appreciated.

Turn right along the tree-lined promenade through Jubilee Gardens, which are protected by covenant, established by Shell, that prohibits any building work on them.

The great white slab of the ❷ **Shell Centre**, international office for the petroleum company, is prominent across the grass on your right. It was designed by Sir Howard Robinson, who also consulted on the United Nations building in New York. Built in 1953-62, the twenty-seven-storey tower, clad in Portland stone, rises to 107m (350ft).

❸ **Hungerford Bridge** was built in 1864 to carry trains between Charing Cross and the south coast. Opened in 2002, the imaginative walkways along each side are strapped onto the foundation piers of the old railway bridge.

Go under the bridge and pass a series of 1950s designed buildings before reaching Waterloo Bridge. Originally this was an area of wharves and factories badly damaged by bombs in World War II. It was revitalised as the site of the Festival of Britain in 1951, marking the centenary of the Great Exhibition in Hyde Park and redefining the South Bank as a major national cultural centre.

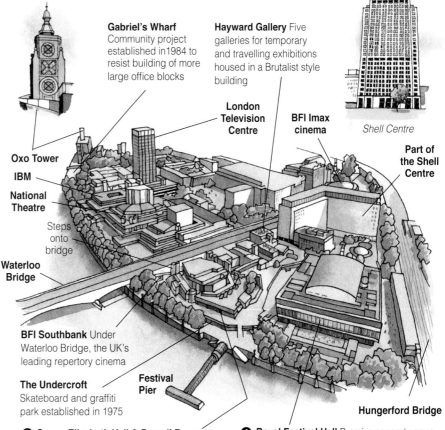

Gabriel's Wharf Community project established in1984 to resist building of more large office blocks

Hayward Gallery Five galleries for temporary and travelling exhibitions housed in a Brutalist style building

London Television Centre

BFI Imax cinema

Shell Centre

Part of the Shell Centre

Oxo Tower

IBM

National Theatre

Steps onto bridge

Waterloo Bridge

BFI Southbank Under Waterloo Bridge, the UK's leading repertory cinema

Festival Pier

The Undercroft Skateboard and graffiti park established in 1975

Hungerford Bridge

❺ **Queen Elizabeth Hall & Purcell Room** Small concert venues with shared foyer. Much criticised Brutalist style buildings. Elizabeth Hall seats 1,000 for concerts. The Purcell Room stages mainly chamber music

❹ **Royal Festival Hall** Premier concert venue. Focal point of the Southbank Centre. Designed by Robert Matthew and Leslie Martin for the 1951 Festival of Britain. Considered one of the best Modernist structures in London

Go under Waterloo Bridge, turn immediately right and climb the steps on to the bridge for a dramatic view of the great bulk of the ❻ **Royal National Theatre** which had a long-drawn-out performance of its own before finally opening in 1976. The foundations were laid in 1951 but financial problems halted progress until 1963 when Sir Denys Lasdun was appointed as architect. Construction eventually began in 1969. His Brutalist design of an assembly of rough-cast concrete blocks and slabs has been much criticised but when the sun casts deep shadows or when it's floodlit at night the monumental construction makes sense.

Head over the bridge towards the north bank. The present smooth cantilevered ❼ **Waterloo Bridge** was opened in 1944, designed by Sir Giles Gilbert Scott, replacing an original dating back to 1817 which threatened to collapse. Situated on a bend in the river, the bridge provides much-admired views along the Thames in both directions, although the view to the city has been tainted in recent years by a rash of discordant skyscrapers.

National Theatre

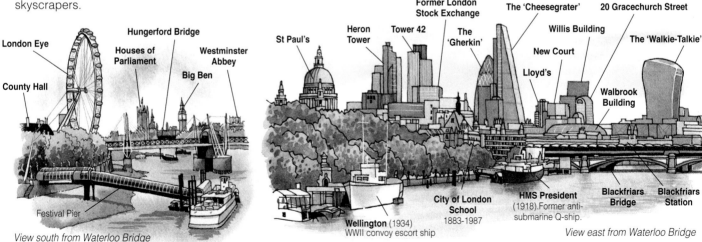

London Eye

County Hall

Hungerford Bridge

Houses of Parliament

Westminster Abbey

Big Ben

St Paul's

Heron Tower

Tower 42

The 'Gherkin'

Former London Stock Exchange

The 'Cheesegrater'

20 Gracechurch Street

Willis Building

New Court

The 'Walkie-Talkie'

Lloyd's

Walbrook Building

Festival Pier

View south from Waterloo Bridge

Wellington (1934) WWII convoy escort ship

City of London School 1883-1987

HMS President (1918).Former anti-submarine Q-ship.

Blackfriars Bridge

Blackfriars Station

View east from Waterloo Bridge

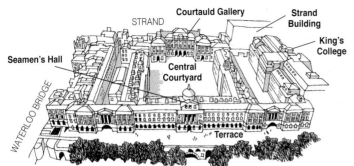

Somerset House

The large neo-Classical building on the north bank is **❽ Somerset House**, one of the most important 18th-century buildings in London. Built on the site of a 16th-century palace it was designed by William Chambers and built in 1775-86 as an early office block for several government departments. Since then admiralty officials have lived and worked there, it has housed various Royal Societies and for a long period most of it was occupied by the Inland Revenue. The river frontage is extremely long – 244m (800ft) – including the extension for King's College. We shall return to Somerset House later...

Across the Strand at the end of Lancaster Place stands **❾ One Aldwych**, built in 1906-7 and designed by Mewès & Davis, who also created the Ritz. They were early pioneers of the steel framework used in this French-style building which is faced with Norwegian granite. It's cleverly designed to follow the curve of the Aldwych on a triangular-shaped footprint and initially housed the *Morning Post* newspaper until being converted to an hotel in 1998.

Go over Lancaster Place at the traffic lights to the left side of the Strand. The second turning on your left leads to the **❿ Savoy Hotel**. It was built in 1889 on the site of the medieval Savoy Palace by impresario Richard D'Oyly Carte with profits from his Gilbert & Sullivan operas, which were performed in his adjoining theatre. The entrance court from the Strand was restyled in 1929 and it famously remains the only street in Britain where traffic drives on the right. Nobody seems quite sure why.

Cross the Strand to Southampton Street, which gently rises between red-brick buildings to Covent Garden.

One Aldwych

The Savoy Hotel

⑪ Covent Garden was originally designed by 17th-century architect Inigo Jones to an Italian model, though the fine buildings around today's square are almost entirely Victorian. Charles Fowler's neo-Classical covered market building was developed on the site of a former walled garden at the centre of the square in 1833. Further development turned Covent Garden into London's main fruit and vegetable wholesale market.

By the end of the 1960s, traffic congestion around the area had become a problem and in 1974 the market relocated. The central building re-opened as a shopping centre in 1980, and is now a hugely popular tourist destination with cafés, bars, small shops, restaurants and market stalls. There are trendy shops around the square and a procession of street entertainers to enjoy. Covent Garden gets extremely busy!

London Transport Museum

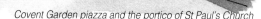
Covent Garden piazza and the portico of St Paul's Church

The **⑫ London Transport Museum** occupies the eastern corner of the square, housed in the picturesque Victorian Flower Market built in 1872.

London's transport is essentially the social history of the capital. Tram, bus and underground route patterns first reflected the city's growth, then began to promote it. The museum has a fine collection of 20th-century poster art in its well-stocked shop.

St Pauls' churchyard

Designed by Inigo Jones, **⑬ St Paul's Church** was consecrated in 1638 and has long been called the 'actors' church'. The main entrance on the square has never been used and access is through a pleasant garden at the west end. The first Punch and Judy show was performed under the portico of St Paul's in 1662 and was recorded by Samuel Pepys in his famous diary.

The Central Market from Russell Street

Floral Hall of the old Covent Garden market. Became part of the Opera House in the 1996-99 renovation

Bow Street Magistrate's Court

'The Young Dancer' by Enzo Plazzotta, erected 1988

Royal Opera House

The **⑭ Royal Opera House** occupies the northern corner of the square, marked by colonnades. To view the famous front façade our route leaves the square along James Street.

Towards the end of the street, on the corner with Long Acre, is Covent Garden tube station, opened in 1907. The building is clad in classic 'oxblood' tiles with art deco lettering above. It's one of the few central London stations which has only stairs or lifts for platform access. Climbing the stairs is the equivalent of a five-storey building. Passenger congestion – and irritation – is common.

Turn right along Long Acre then first right into Bow Street. The giant six-column portico of the Opera House is ahead.

The first theatre on the Royal Opera House site was built in 1732, but it burnt down in 1808 and a subsequent building suffered the same fate in 1855. The façade, foyer and auditorium of the present Opera House were designed by Edward Barry in 1858, but almost every other part of the complex came from a huge reconstruction in the 1990s.

It's been the home of The Royal Opera since 1945 and the Royal Ballet since 1946. All the world's greatest singers and dancers have performed at 'Covent Garden', one of the world's leading opera houses.

The first court in **⑮ Bow Street**, then a notorious gin-soaked area, was established in a private house in 1784. The novelist Henry Fielding, who served as a magistrate, established the 'Bow Street Runners', Britain's first paid police force, to tackle the crime and disorder in the district.

The 'official' Magistrates' Court building was completed in 1881 and closed in 2006. Famous defendants who appeared there on their way to higher courts include Casanova, Dr Crippen, the Kray twins, General Pinochet and Oscar Wilde.

Tavistock Street

In medieval times this area was a garden that supplied Westminster Abbey with produce. These days the narrow streets are an attractive blend of small shops, pubs, coffee houses and restaurants, and a peaceful antidote to the crowds usually thronging the central piazza.

Continue down Bow Street and turn left along Russell Street to the **⓰ Theatre Royal, Drury Lane**.

London's 18th-century theatres regularly burnt down and the Theatre Royal is the fourth on this site. Designed by Benjamin Wyatt and others in 1810, the porch and Ionic colonnade along Russell Street were added in 1831. The theatre is surprisingly large, both outside and in, and still has its early 19th-century decoration.

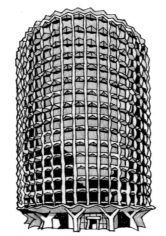

One Kemble Street

Cross Drury Lane and continue straight on into Kemble Street. On the corner with Kingsway stands the Space House, an unloved legacy of the 1960s property boom. Designed by Richard Seifert, who was also responsible for Centre Point, the façade of the stubby, sixteen-storey tower has an intricate façade of precast cruciform blocks. Now renamed **⓱ One Kemble Street** the tower has a number of tenants, including the Government Legal Department.

Go right into Kingsway, opened in 1905 as part of a major north-south route through central London. **⓲ Bush House** is the focal point where it joins the Aldwych. Built in imposing neo-Classical style as a trade centre by an American, Irving T. Bush, and completed in 1935, Bush House is graced with various statues symbolising Anglo-American relations. The BBC World Service was located here until it moved to the new extension at Broadcasting House in 2012.

Turn right to walk round the beautiful sweep of the Aldwych, then go left into the Strand with the entrance to Somerset House across the road on your right.

Bush House

Seen from the Strand the attractive triple-arched gatehouse of ❽ **Somerset House** occupies only a third of the total site width. For many years Somerset House was closed to the public but during the 1990s it was transformed into an art and cultural centre. The central courtyard was cleared of car parking, repaved and 55 dancing fountains installed. It's now the venue for concerts and theatre in the summer, with Christmas festivities and ice skating in the winter.

In 1990 London University's Courtauld Institute moved into the building and the celebrated Courtauld Gallery occupies a refurbished suite of rooms in the section overlooking the Strand, once home to the Royal Academy of Art. The gallery has one of the best collections of art anywhere in Europe, particularly major works by the Impressionists and Post-Impressionists.

Somerset House courtyard

King's College archway

The East Wing is part of the campus of ❿ **King's College London**, with a handsome building designed by Robert Smirke in 1829.

Especially fine is the arch leading from the courtyard to the terrace, where there's a well-regarded restaurant with fabulous views overlooking the river. The front of the college facing the Strand is an inferior 1960s addition.

St Mary-le-Strand

Return to the Strand where ⓴ **St Mary-le-Strand** church stands marooned in the middle of one of the city's busiest thoroughfares. It's one of two 'island' churches in this street (St Clement Danes is the other). Built in English Baroque style in 1714-17, it was the first major public project for James Gibbs who later went on to design St Martin-in-the-Fields.

Born a Roman Catholic in Scotland, Gibbs received his architectural training in Italy. His initial designs were considered too Italianate for the Protestant church commissioners so Gibbs, with a nod to Christopher Wren, added the 'wedding cake' steeple.

Turn right off the Strand down nearby Surrey Street which takes you to the riverside and Temple tube station, the end of this walk.

Holborn & The Temple

Places of interest

❶ St Clement Danes
❷ Royal Courts of Justice
❸ Twinings
❹ Temple Bar
❺ Carey Street
❻ The Seven Stars
❼ Sir Thomas More statue
❽ Royal College of Surgeons
❾ Saw Swee Hock Student Centre
❿ Old Curiosity Shop
⓫ Lincoln's Inn Fields
⓬ Lindsey House
⓭ Newcastle House
⓮ Sir John Soane's Museum
⓯ Lincoln's Inn
⓰ The Law Society
⓱ Prince Henry's Room
⓲ The Temple
⓳ Temple Church
⓴ Temple Gardens

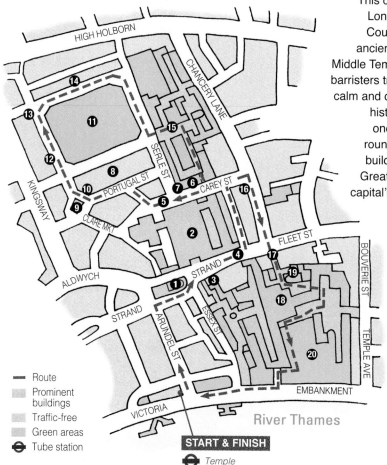

— Route
▒ Prominent buildings
▒ Traffic-free
▒ Green areas
⊖ Tube station

START & FINISH
⊖ Temple

This circular walk visits the heart of London's legal system: the Royal Courts of Justice and three of the ancient Inns of Court; Lincoln's Inn, Middle Temple and Inner Temple, where barristers train and then practise. This is calm and dignified London, packed with history and interest. There's also one of the world's only surviving round churches and other ancient buildings which predate London's Great Fire of 1666, plus one of the capital's earliest residential squares.

Note
The Inns of Court are closed at weekends, so this walk needs to be done during the week.

START & FINISH: Temple tube station.
LENGTH: 2 miles approx, on busy streets. Some gentle slopes.
REFRESHMENTS: In the Strand and Fleet Street. Sparse elsewhere.

THE WALK

From Temple tube station walk up Arundel Street and turn right into the Strand, an upper class enclave in the 17th century, then famous for its coffee shops, taverns and music halls. ❶ **St Clement Danes** church is in front of you, marooned on an island among the traffic. Designed by Christopher Wren, the church was completed in 1682. Its Portland stone tower and open spire topped by a dome and turret were added by James Gibbs in 1719. Now the central church of the Royal Air Force, it claims to be the church featured in the nursery rhyme Oranges and Lemons, as the bells play this tune.

St Clement Danes

Beyond the church are the ❷ **Royal Courts of Justice**, commonly called the Law Courts, housing the Court of Appeal of England and Wales and the High Court of Justice of England and Wales. They are the nation's main civil courts dealing with cases such as divorce, libel, and appeals. Criminal cases are dealt with at the Old Bailey nearby.

The building, said to be the 'last great Gothic public building in London', is a sprawling and fanciful edifice designed by George Edmund Street, a solicitor turned architect who died in 1881 exhausted by his efforts. Opened by Queen Victoria in 1882, it connects Lincoln's Inn with the Temples as a continuous bastion of the British legal system. The Law Courts are said to contain some 1,000 rooms with 3.5 miles of corridors and 88 separate courtrooms. TV crews and protesters are a familiar sight outside, waiting for verdicts to be delivered.

The extensive Royal Courts of Justice

Royal Courts of Justice

❸ Twinings opened in 1716 opposite the Law Courts, the first ever 'dry' (no alcohol) tea and coffee shop in the city. It banned alcohol in order to appeal to ladies. The company now sells every kind of specialist tea. The famous doorway dates from 1787 when, ironically, the shop was a pub called the Golden Lion.

Twinings

❹ Temple Bar stands where the Strand narrows into Fleet Street, marking the western entrance to the City of London. Originally the Bar was marked by an archway designed by Christopher Wren which was removed during road widening in 1878 and replaced by a slimmer Bar, topped by a griffin in 1880. Traditionally the Monarch has to pause here and ask the Lord Mayor for permission to enter the City.

Turn left into narrow Bell Yard alongside the law courts. At the top turn left into **❺ Carey Street**, once the location for bankruptcy courts and the creation of the phrase 'In Carey Street', or corrupted to 'Queer street' – slang for being bankrupt. This area was once a teeming warren of yards and narrow lanes populated by the Victorian poor, memorably depicted in the novels of

Temple Bar

Charles Dickens. The slums have long gone but the street is still rich in bygone character.

❻ The Seven Stars is dated 1602 and was formerly known as The Log and Seven Stars. A favourite haunt of legal folk, the pub faces the back of the law courts. Numerous caricatures of barristers and judges line the red-painted walls of the two main rooms and there are posters of legal-themed British films, big ceiling fans and checked tablecloths that add a quirky, almost continental touch. The toilet facilities are notoriously novel.

The shop next door used to sell wigs for judges and barristers and still retains its original frontage with a display of its former merchandise in the window.

Further along on the corner of Serle Street there's a statue of **❼ Sir Thomas More**, 'some time Lord High Chancellor of England', sculpted in 1886 by Robert Smith and set in a red brick niche above one of the entrances to Lincoln's Inn where More was a student.

The Seven Stars

Sir Thomas More statue

Continue along Carey Street then turn left into Portugal Street. Facing you is the rear of the **❽ Royal College of Surgeons**, built by Charles Barry, which houses the remarkable collection of 18th-century surgeon and scientist, John Hunter.

Further along Portugal Street you come to the striking **❾ Saw Swee Hock Student Union**, designed by the Dublin practice O'Donnell & Tuomey in 2013. It's an energetic, restless building in red brick, set at crazy angles and squeezed onto a triangular site, part of the London School of Economics. With seven storeys above ground and two beneath, the building is named after an alumnus who donated £2.5 million to fund the construction.

Its strident modernity is emphasised by being only 20 metres across the street from the **❿ Old Curiosity Shop**, a genuine 17th-century building, that survived the Great Fire of 1666 and probably the oldest shop in central London.

It's unlikely to have been the inspiration for Charles Dickens to write the novel of the same name, but he possibly knew the building and it would have been pretty old then.

Saw Swee Hock Student Union

The Old Curiosity Shop

Keep straight on, climbing slightly, into the wide open spaces of **⓫ Lincoln's Inn Fields**, once a public execution site and now one of central London's largest public spaces. In Stuart and Tudor times many religious martyrs and those convicted of treachery against the state perished here.

This was London's first garden square, laid out by property developer William Newton in 1640. The central garden is now planted with plane trees and is a popular sun trap with tennis courts and a café. Mid-17th-century brick houses overlook two sides, with the Royal College of Surgeons almost filling the south and the east appropriated by Lincoln's Inn.

Lindsey House

Walk up the left side of the square which is lined by substantial houses set back from the road.

⑫ Lindsey House, now divided into two, numbers 59-60, is the only remaining original house in the square. It's in the style of Inigo Jones but the authorship is disputed. Spencer Percival, the only British prime minister to have been assassinated, once lived here (he was shot by John Bellingham in 1812).

⑬ Newcastle House at the top corner of the square replaced an original mansion that burnt down in 1684. Today's version has been much altered but still retains the good looks of the 17th-century replacement. Two rear wings were demolished in the early 1900s for the development of Kingsway, the major highway running alongside the square.

The Duke of Newcastle preferred to live here rather than in Downing Street when he had two spells as prime minister in 1754-56 and 1757-62. Farrer and Co, solicitors to the Royal family, have occupied the building since 1790.

Newcastle House

Turn right along the top of the square to **⑭ Sir John Soane's Museum**, the former home of the architect responsible for the Bank of England and now one of the most surprising museums in London, displaying his quirky collection of art, archaeology and other intriguing items.

Left to the nation on his death in 1837, Soane stipulated that nothing should be changed. His request has been gloriously maintained. The three large houses are themselves a kaleidoscope of architectural surprises and illusions, and the collection includes the series of Hogarth's oils for the the engravings of the *Rake's Progress* and Soane's original designs for the Bank of England.

Sir John Soane's Museum

The Gatehouse

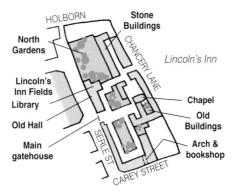

HOLBORN

Stone Buildings

North Gardens

CHANCERY LANE

Lincoln's Inn

Lincoln's Inn Fields

Library

Old Hall

Main gatehouse

SERLE ST

Chapel

Old Buildings

Arch & bookshop

CAREY STREET

⓯ Lincoln's Inn is one of the ancient four Inns of court where barristers lodge, train and then practise. The other three are Grey's Inn (north of High Holborn), Inner Temple and Middle Temple, which we will visit later in the walk.

The origins of the inns are unclear but can be attributed to a 13th-century Dominican Friary which became a hostel for lawyers. The Inns are made up of buildings of all ages picturesquely arranged like colleges at Oxford or Cambridge Universities.

Go through the mock-Tudor gatehouse and step back in time exploring this delightful area.

The Old Hall (1494), distinctive with diamond-patterned brickwork and tudor chimneys, is on your left. The Court of Chancery sat here from 1835-58 and it used to be the living room of the resident lawyers. The distant Stone Buildings (1774-80) is one of London's best examples of Palladianism in a public building. The stone Chapel (1619-23) has an unusual vaulted undercroft made up of gravestones and the Old Buildings are a delightful gathering of 16th-century turreted brick houses.

Turn right into New Square, a well-preserved U-shape of four-storey terraces housing lawyers' chambers. Return to Carey Street through an ornamental archway where Wildy & Sons have been selling lawbooks since 1830.

The library, Old Hall and gatehouse

Wildy & Sons Bookshop

Ede & Ravenscroft's window

Continue left along Carey Street. Before reaching Chancery Lane take a short detour into Star Yard to the rear of Ede & Ravenscroft's, suppliers of robes and made-to-measure wigs to barristers. There's usually a splendid display of their wares in the window.

16 The Law Society building, headquarters of the solicitors' professional body, dominates the corner of Carey Street with Chancery Lane. Completed in 1831 by Lewis Vulliamy with a corner extension in 1902 by Charles Holden, its grand neo-Classical façade seems wasted in this narrow street. Golden lions on the railings were rescued from the British Museum.

Opposite is the former Public Record Office built by James Pennethorne in 1851-66, with the Chancery Lane extension by John Taylor in 1891-6. Public records were moved to Kew in 1997 and the building now houses King's College London's Maughan Library.

A Law Society golden lion

Continue down Chancery Lane. Across Fleet Street ahead is the beautiful half-timbered **17 Prince Henry's Room**, built in 1610 as a tavern, which miraculously escaped the Great Fire of 1666.

The name refers to the coat of arms and the initials PH in the centre of a fine Jacobean ceiling, probably in honour of James I's eldest son, Henry, who died at the age of 16 before he became king.

The house is built over the entrance to the Inner Temple, through which you should walk to enjoy the rarefied atmosphere within.

Prince Henry's Room

The Law Society

During the Middle Ages **⓲ The Temple** was part of a monastery of military monks, known as the Knights Templar, who fought the Crusades to protect Christian pilgrims in the Holy Land. The order was suppressed in the 14th century and its premises taken over by lawyers. The section outside the jurisdiction of the City of London became the 'Outer Temple' and the remainder the 'Inner Temple'. The distinction is less clear these days but both share Temple Church as their joint chapel.

The lane from Fleet Street goes through an avenue of lawyers' chambers leading to **⓳ Temple Church**, built for the Knights Templar in the12th Century. Like other churches they built throughout Europe it's based on the circular design of the Church of the Holy Sepulchre in Jerusalem. The original 18m (59ft) diameter round church now acts as the nave after the rectangular section was built on approximately half a century later, forming the chancel. Initiations to the order probably took place in the church, where life-sized effigies of knights are now laid out in the ancient nave.

Temple Church

A 10m (33ft) high column outside the church was erected in 2000. The bronze statue on the top depicts a horse with two riders, derived from the seal of the knights who were originally too poor to have a horse each. The column also marks the spot where the Great Fire of 1666 was extinguished.

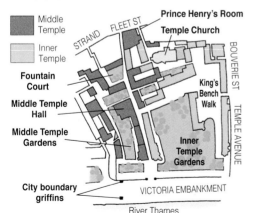

Middle Temple
Inner Temple
STRAND FLEET ST
Prince Henry's Room
Temple Church
BOUVERIE ST
Fountain Court
King's Bench Walk
Middle Temple Hall
TEMPLE AVENUE
Middle Temple Gardens
Inner Temple Gardens
City boundary griffins
VICTORIA EMBANKMENT
River Thames

Go through an archway at the east end of the church into King's Bench Walk, a wide street of 17th-century red-brick buildings. Then turn right into the first of the **⓴ Temple Gardens** which run down to the Thames embankment, covering some three acres.

Much of this area was rebuilt after extensive bomb damage during WWII but it still retains the relaxed ambience of a pre-war red-brick university. The labyrinth of narrow lanes, alleys, courts and passageways can seem almost as complex and confusing as the English legal system itself. The best way to enjoy it is just take a relaxed stroll around, but don't miss Middle Temple Hall, built in 1563-73 replacing an earlier one. It's one of the finest Elizabethan halls in Britain with a double hammer beam roof and was the venue for the first performance of Shakespeare's *Twelfth Night*. There's also a fountain in Fountain Court which dates to 1681.

Leave the Temple through the gateway onto Victoria Embankment. Turn right past the two roadside griffins marking the City boundary. The walk ends where it began at Temple tube station.

St Paul's & Bankside

Places of interest

1. Central Criminal Court
2. St Martin, Ludgate Hill
3. St Paul's Cathedral
4. Temple Bar
5. Paternoster Square
6. Millennium Bridge
7. Tate Modern
8. Bankside Galley
9. Cardinal's Wharf
10. Shakespeare's Globe
11. Southwark Bridge
12. Vintner's Hall
13. Five Kings House
14. St James Garlickhithe
15. Albert Buildings
16. Bracken House
17. St Nicholas Cove Abbey
18. College of Arms
19. St Augustine Church
20. One New Change

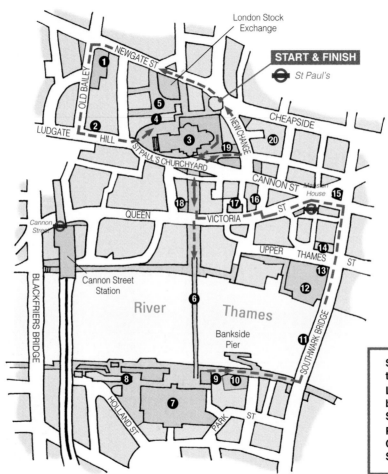

This circular walk visits three of London's most iconic and historic buildings: St Paul's Cathedral; the Central Criminal Court (Old Bailey); and Tate Modern, a power station conversion. It also includes a crossing of the Millennium Bridge which has quickly become another must-see favourite. There's much to enjoy on this route and fabulous views from the two bridges crossed.

— Route
▨ Prominent buildings
▨ Traffic-free
▨ Green areas
🚇 Tube station

START & FINISH: St Paul's tube station.
LENGTH: 2 miles approx, on busy streets. Gentle slopes. Steps onto Southwark Bridge.
REFRESHMENTS: St Paul's Churchyard, Tate Modern, Salvation Army.

THE WALK

Leave St Paul's tube station and turn left along Newgate Street. Pass the London Stock Exchange which transferred here from Bishopsgate in 2004. As the street widens and opposite St Sepulchre's Church, turn left around the great, grey building of the ❶ **Central Criminal Court**, commonly called the Old Bailey after the narrow street in which it stands.

Designed in bold, neo-Baroque style by Edward William Mountford and built 1900-07, it replaced the infamous Newgate Prison where the last public hanging in Britain took place in 1868. The original building had another seven bays which were destroyed in the Blitz. They were replaced by the South Block, built in 1968 & 1972, designed by architects Donald McMorran and George Whitby.

The Old Bailey site has been the venue for many famous trials since 1539. These days it deals with major criminal cases for the London area. Its 18 courts, packed on the first floor, handle around 1,700 cases a year.

British sculptor F.W. Pomeroy designed the famous bronze statue *Lady Justice* on top of the dome. She carries the sword of strength in one hand and the scales of justice in the other.

Continue down Old Bailey and turn left into Ludgate Hill, one of the three ancient hills of London, the others being Tower Hill and Cornhill.

The sombre-looking church on your left is ❷ **St Martin, Ludgate Hill**, built in Baroque style by Christopher Wren during 1777-87 to replace a medieval one destroyed in the Great Fire. A lead-covered octagonal cupola supports a balcony and the tapered spire rises to a height of 48m (158ft). The famous view of St Paul's up the hill has been spoilt by the intrusion of Juxon House, built in the 1960s.

St Martin, Ludgate Hill

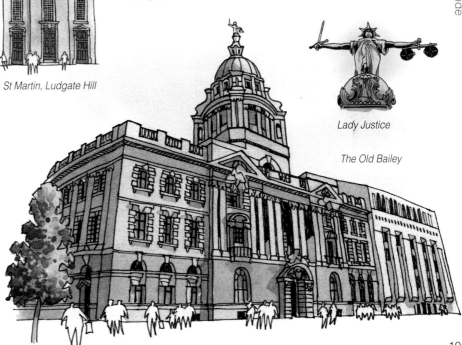

Lady Justice

The Old Bailey

St Paul's from Ludgate Hill

❸ **St Paul's** is the fifth cathedral to adorn Ludgate Hill, the first being a wooden building founded in 604. The fourth, the largest in Britain at the time, with a 489m (149ft) spire, was burnt to the ground in the Great Fire of 1666.

Christopher Wren was commissioned to rebuild it, a task completed in 1710 when Wren was 78 years old and 35 years after the final design was agreed. Wren's initial Great Model of 1672 was unpopular with the authorities and what we see today is a watered-down compromise.

The famous dome was inspired by St Peter's Basilica in Rome, rising 108m (365ft) to the cross at its summit. The Whispering Gallery runs around the inside, 30m (99ft) above the cathedral floor and is reached by 259 steps from ground level. It's so named because a whisper against its wall is audible all round the gallery.

The twin towers at the western end were not part of Wren's original plans but he added them in 1707. Each was designed to hold a clock.

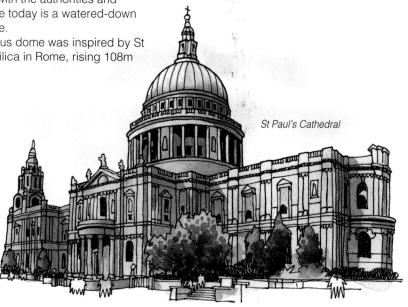

St Paul's Cathedral

Inside, St Paul's is remarkably spacious, cool and well ordered. The Baroque splendour beneath the massive 31m (102ft) diameter dome has been the scene of many great national events, amongst them the funeral of Winston Churchill in 1965 and the wedding of Prince Charles and Lady Diana Spencer in 1981.

Ironically, a specially introduced coal tax funded the new cathedral, replacing the one destroyed by fire. The cathedral miraculously survived the capital's second great inferno, the Blitz, during World War II.

Continue into St Paul's Churchyard, which used to be the centre of London's book trade. 'Churchyard' is a loose term for the precincts of a cathedral, rather than a burial ground.

❹ **Temple Bar**, the only surviving gateway into the City of London is on your left. The handsome Portland stone archway has a chequered history. First erected by Charles II at the junction of Fleet Street and the Strand in 1671, the monument was dismantled in 1878 when it began to impede traffic flow. No other site could be found and it spent more than a century on the Hertfordshire estate of the brewer, Sir Henry Meux. After a long campaign by the Temple Bar Trust, the Bar was returned to the City in 2004 and reconstructed as a magnificent entrance to Paternoster Square.

Temple Bar

During 1996-2003, William Whitfield's masterplan converted ❺ **Paternoster Square** from a rather grim 1960s eyesore into a bright and vibrant area of shops, offices and restaurants. The main monument in the central piazza is a 23m (75ft) tall Corinthian column of Portland stone topped by a flaming copper urn covered in gold leaf. It's illuminated by fibre-optic lighting at night and sometimes referred to as the 'pineapple'.

Walk around the eastern end of the cathedral, a pleasant green area with trees and seats, usually busy at lunchtimes with dark-suited office workers.

Paternoster Square

Cross the busy road at the lights and walk down Peter's Hill to the ❻ **Millennium Bridge**. After it began to sway when pedestrians crossed at the grand opening in 2000, the bridge was extensively modified at a cost of some £5 million and reopened in 2002. The handsome steel suspension footbridge, built by the Arup Group, with Foster and Partners, and Sir Anthony Caro, crosses the Thames from St Paul's to Tate Modern, providing wonderful panoramic views along the way.

The Millennium Bridge

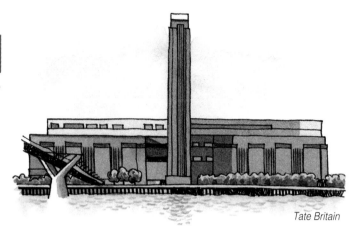

Tate Britain

Cross the Millennium Bridge to ❼ **Tate Modern**, housed in the former Bankside power station, the most visited modern art gallery in the world with around 4.7 million visitors a year. It was established in 2000, designed by J. Herzog and de Meuron with a permanent collection consisting of international works from 1900 onwards and several more galleries housing temporary exhibitions.

The power station closed in 1981 and the the vast Turbine Hall, designed by Sir Giles Gilbert Scott, architect of Battersea Power Station, now displays large specially-commissioned works by contemporary artists, often generating popular media controversy. Extensions to the original buildings were opened in 2012 and 2016. Naturally, both were controversial.

If more traditional art is your preference, head for the excellent ❽ **Bankside Gallery** nearby. It's the headquarters of two historic bodies, the Royal Watercolour Society and Royal Society of Painter-Printmakers, and displays contemporary watercolours. The Founder's Arms, a handy hostelry beside the Thames, was built on the site of the foundry where the bells of St Paul's were cast. The view of the cathedral from here is sensational.

Cardinal's Wharf

Retrace your steps back to the Tate and join the popular walk along the riverside. ❾ **Cardinal's Wharf** is a small group of remarkably preserved 17th-century houses in the shadow of Tate Modern. A plaque claims that Christopher Wren stayed in one of the houses while St Paul's was being built. The name comes from Cardinal Wolsey, Bishop of Winchester in 1529 who lived in nearby Winchester Palace when in London.

This area was once the Soho of its day, known for entertainment and bawdy houses. Some of that lusty 16th-century theatre is recreated in ❿ **Shakespeare's Globe**, founded by the pioneering American actor and director Sam Wanamaker. It opened in 1997, near to the site of the original theatre which burnt down in 1613. The centre of the circular wood and thatch structure is open to the elements, so public performances on the outdoor stage are restricted to the summer months.

Shakespeare's Globe

Replacing an earlier structure, **⑪ Southwark Bridge** was built in 1912-21 with Ernest George as architect and Basil Mott as engineer. The five steel arches, painted yellow and green, are supported on granite piers. At 73m (240ft) wide, the centre arch is the longest cast iron span ever made.

Southwark Bridge

Climb the steps onto the bridge from where there are terrific views up and down the river with the **⑫ Vintners' Hall** on the northern bank looking particularly fine. There's been a hall on this site since 1446. One was destroyed in the Great Fire and the present building dates to the 1670s with various additions and modifications since.

One of London's 12 livery companies, the Worshipful Company of Vintners originally controlled the wine trade in England. Nearby Garlickhythe was a dock where French garlic and wine were landed from medieval times. London's livery companies play a significant part in City life, charity fund-raising and providing networking opportunities.

Vintners' Hall

The doorway of Five Kings House

St James Garlickhythe

⑬ Five Kings House was originally the northern end of Thames House, built for Liebig's Extract of Meat Company by Stanley Hamp in 1911, but was divided off in 1990. The ornate doorway on the corner of Upper Thames Street grabs the attention at street level but the rest of this prodigious Edwardian Baroque building is worth appraisal too.

⑭ St James Garlickhythe, across the road, is another Christopher Wren church, built in 1674-87 with the steeple added in 1713. The church was nicknamed 'Wren's lantern' owing to its profusion of windows. Wren redesigned 53 City churches after the Great Fire, 23 of which survive.

Cross Upper Thames at the traffic lights and head straight up Queen Street. Turn left when you reach Cannon Street then left again into Queen Victoria Street. Pause at Mansion House tube station to admire **15 Albert Buildings** across the road, a cheery Victorian office block, built in 1869, designed by Frederick J Ward.

Albert Buildings

Keep left along the broad sweep of Queen Victoria Street, crossing to the right at the lights to **16 Bracken House**, a late example of modern classicism, constructed on a cleared bomb site between 1955-58, designed by Sir Albert Richardson as the headquarters and printing works of the *Financial Times*.

Bracken House

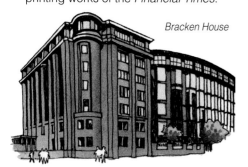

17 St Nicholas Cole Abbey next door is a Christopher Wren rebuild during 1671-7 after the original 12th-century building was destroyed in the Great Fire. The church suffered substantial bomb damage during the London Blitz in World War II and

St Nicholas Cole Abbey

was reconstructed by Arthur Bailey in 1961–2. Curiously, it has never been an abbey, the name derives from a medieval word for a traveller's shelter.

Further along, across the street, is the sleek glass international headquarters of the Salvation Army built by Sheppard Robson in 2005. Funded by selling off part of the site, it features a huge café on the ground floor.

Before turning right onto Peter's Hill and walking back to St Paul's, take a look at the **18 College of Arms** at the junction.

The elegant 17th-century building, home of the royal heralds, was designed by a master bricklayer and is a good example of the 'artisan style'.

The college was granted a charter in 1484 and is still active, examining and recording pedigrees and granting coats of arms. The magnificent black and gilded iron gates to the courtyard were transferred here from Goodrich Court, Herefordshire in 1956.

College of Arms

Peter's Hill returns you to St Paul's. The futuristic, low building across the grass on your left, dramatically different to the cathedral, is the City Information Point designed by Make Architects in 2008.

Cross the road into St Paul's churchyard and work your way round to what remains of ⑲ **St Augustine Church** which was devastated by bombing in World War II.

The original church was built by Christopher Wren during 1677-87 but isn't considered to be his finest work. The tower, possibly the best part, survived and was incorporated into the 1960s Choir School of the Cathedral.

St Augustine Church

Reflections of St Paul's in One New Change

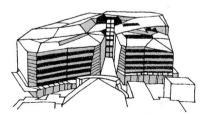

One New Change from St Paul's

⑳ **One New Change** was built in 2011 by Jean Nouvel in a bid to bring the retail, restaurant and café experience to this part of the city. Providing 20,500sqm of retail space and 30,700sqm for offices over eight storeys, it's a fairly standard shopping mall, glass clad and with the now obligatory viewing plaftorm. A 'slot' on the western side cleverly orients the building towards the dome of St Paul's, creating a kaleidoscope of magical reflections of the cathedral in the glass walls. A 12m (39ft) tall sculpture of a rusty nail set at a crooked angle by Gavin Turk stands at the end of the 'slot' adding a further surreal aspect to the scene.

To end the walk head north along New Change into Cheapside and St Paul's tube station.

WALK 12

The City

Places of interest

1. Bank of England
2. Royal Exchange
3. Guildhall
4. St Lawrence Jewry
5. St Mary-le-Bow
6. Mansion House
7. No 1 Poultry
8. St Stephen Walbrook
9. New Court
10. The Walbrook Building
11. Cannon Place
12. The Monument
13. Leadenhall Market
14. 20 Fenchurch Street
15. Lloyd's
16. Willis Building
17. Leadenhall Building
18. St Helen's
19. 30 St Mary Axe
20. St Andrew Undershaft
21. St Helen's Bishopsgate
22. Heron Tower
23. St Ethelburga the Virgin
24. Tower 42
25. Gibson Hall
26. St Mary Woolnoth

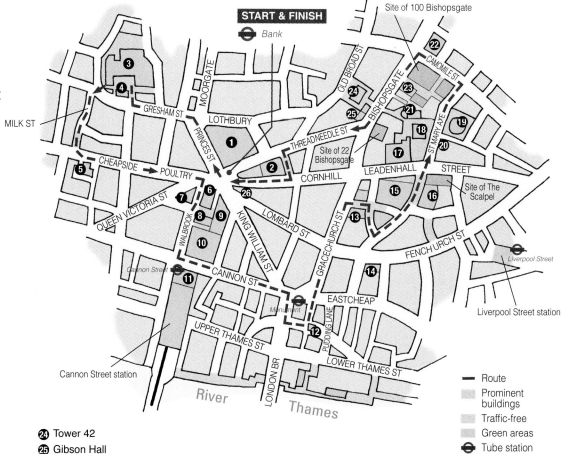

Built on the site of the original Roman settlement, London's financial centre, the City, is also a treasure house of riches for students of architecture.

Apart from its famous historic buildings, the Square Mile can now also boast the work of five winners of the prestigious Pritzker prize, a density of architectural stardust unequalled anywhere else in the world.

This walk takes in buildings ancient and modern, dour and glossy, short and amazingly tall, as it's the dramatic contrasts that give the City of London its unique character.

START & FINISH: Bank tube station.
LENGTH: 2.5 miles approx, on busy streets. No steps or steep hills.
REFRESHMENTS: Plentiful throughout, though many City eateries and pubs are closed at weekends. Leadenhall Market is only open on weekdays.

THE WALK

Emerge from Bank tube station and pause to take in the remarkable surroundings, once the world's greatest concentrations of wealth and

Former London Stock Exchange opened 1970, 100m (328ft) tall. The Stock Exchange moved to new premises in Paternoster Square in 2004.

❶ Bank of England Only the street walls remain of Sir John Soane's 1788 monumental design. Enlarged in the 1920s & 30s. Central bank of the UK economy established in 1694 to act as banker for the government. 'The Old Lady of Threadneedle Street' issues banknotes in England and Wales.

Duke of Wellington statue 1844 by Francis Leggatt Chantrey.

influence. The trio of ancient neo-Classical buildings are now overlooked by the glittering glass symbols of the modern City, which we will explore later in the walk.

❷ Royal Exchange Trading dates back to 1565. Present building 1844 by Sir William Tite has a Corinthian portico with Roman lettering and sculpture in the pediment. Luxurious shopping centre since 1939.

❻ Mansion House See page 115

❷❹ Tower 42 See page 121

❶❼ Leadenhall Building See page 118

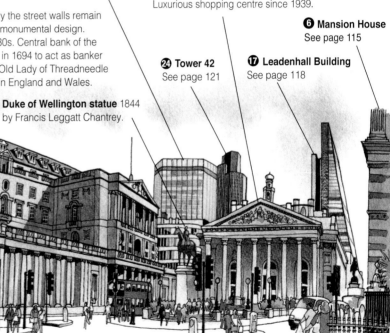

The traditional heart of the City

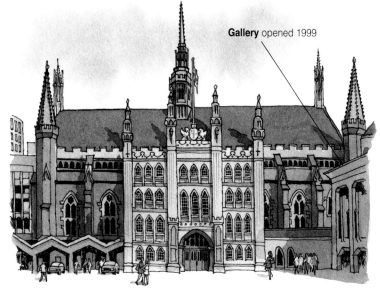

Gallery opened 1999

Guildhall

Begin walking down Princes Street alongside the windowless wall of the Bank of England from where the massive bulk of the building can be appreciated. At the end turn left along Gresham Street to the opening on your right for a wonderful view of the ❸ **Guildhall** across a patterned square.

Dating from 1411, this rather quirky building escaped the Great Fire and is thought to have been where citizens came at one time to pay their taxes. It's no longer the headquarters of the Corporation of London and is now used mainly for ceremonial functions.

The adjacent gallery houses works dating mainly from the 17th century but also Victorian times, and stands on the remains of London's only Roman Amphitheatre, unearthed in 1988.

❹ **St Lawrence Jewry**, the large church opposite the Guildhall, was built in 1670-87 by Christopher Wren. The tower at the east end has a lead-covered Baroque steeple. In medieval times it stood in the Jewish part of the City – hence its name – and was restored after World War II bombing.

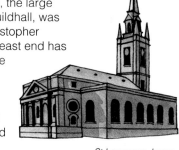

St Lawrence Jewry

Continue along Milk Street, a narrow canyon between modern glass buildings, into Cheapside.

To your left is ❺ **St Mary-le-Bow** church, rebuilt by Sir Christopher Wren in 1670-80 after the Great Fire, with one of his characteristic 'wedding cake' steeples. The church was bombed in 1941 leaving only the steeple and two outer walls standing, but was restored in 1951-62. It's said that only those born within the sound of Bow bells can claim to be true Cockneys.

Cheapside was the site of an important produce market in medieval London. Many of the streets feeding into it are named after the produce that was once sold there, including Honey Lane, Milk Street, Bread Street and Poultry.

St Mary-le-Bow

Cheapside returns you to the start of the walk outside the **❻ Mansion House**, official residence of the Lord Mayor, built in 1753 to the design of George Dance the Elder. The Palladian façade pays tribute to Roman Classicism with six Corinthian columns supporting a broad portico.

Turn left past the Mansion House into Walbrook with **❼ Number One Poultry** on your right, opened in 1998 and designed by Stirling & Wilford. Shaped like a ship on a triangular site, it's one of London's most controversial post-modern buildings. Vividly striped in red and buff sandstone, it encompasses a Conran rooftop restaurant, shops and an entrance to Bank tube station.

Mansion House

Number One Poultry

Queen Victoria St

The **❿ Walbrook Building**, built in 2011 by Foster & Partners, resembles a large-scale wire sculpture; the cladding designed to keep the building cool in summer and warm in winter.

Between the church and the Walbrook Building there's the perfect antidote to modern flashiness: the discreet Queen Anne-style frontage of the Walbrook Club, a private dining establishment.

The Walbrook Club

New Court

Mansion House

Walbrook Building

St Stephen Walbrook

Ahead is **❽ St Stephen Walbrook,** one of the finest of Christopher Wren's City churches, built in 1672-9. The beautiful dome is thought to be Wren's tryout for the one on St Paul's.

Two notable modern buildings overlook St Stephen's. **❾ New Court** is the City HQ of Rothschild Bank, built in 2011 and designed by Rem Koolhaas's OMA. Discreet yet opulent, it's basically a pile of three cubes but much praised by architectural critics.

Continue past the bulbous Walbrook Building into Cannon Street, where there's another assault on your aesthetic senses – **⓫ Cannon Place**, built by Foggo Associates in 2012.

With a total of 36,000sqm of office space over eight floors, the megastructure throbs with machismo. Amazingly, it was built over busy Cannon Street station without any disruption to train services.

Cannon Place

Turn left up Cannon Street then right along King William Street for a look at **⑫ The Monument**, designed by Sir Christopher Wren and Robert Hooke from 1671-76 to commemorate the Great Fire in 1666 and situated close to where it started in Pudding Lane.

Built of Portland stone and 62m (205ft) high, it's the tallest isolated stone column in the world. It's fluted in Roman Doric order and topped by a blazing urn. There's a viewing platform accessed by climbing 311 steps inside the column. The 360 degree views make the climb worthwhile, though possibly not if you're claustrophobic.

The Gracechurch Street entrance to Leadenhall Market

Leadenhall Market

Retrace your steps along King William Street and bear right to cross Cannon Street into Gracechurch Street. Climb the slope and go into **⑬ Leadenhall Market**.

There's been a market here since the Middle Ages. The present ornate covered shopping and restaurant precinct was designed in 1881 by Sir Horace Jones, who also designed Billingsgate Fish Market. It's in a cross-plan layout of the old street configuration.

The main entrance off Gracechurch Street has fluted columns in dark red and cream paintwork, a colour scheme that is continued throughout the lavish interior.

The Monument

20 Fenchurch Street

Lime Street and 'The Walkie-Talkie'

Turn right at the crossroads in the market and leave by the Lime Street exit. You'll be 'rewarded' by a view of the 'Walkie-Talkie' at ⓮ **20 Fenchurch Street** looming threateningly over the older buildings in Lime Street.

Top-heavy buildings usually have an overbearing quality and this one is no exception. The sheer mass of the faceless monster is awesome.

Designed by Rafael Vinoly and built in 2014 the building faced fierce criticism when it was first proposed in 2004. Rising to 160m (525ft) with a total of 55,000 sqm of floor space over 34 storeys, it continues to divide opinion, not helped by the media storm in 2013 when the concentrated rays of the sun reflecting off the curved glass façade set fire to a parked car and a journalist fried an egg using solar energy.

The Willis and Lloyd's Buildings

Turn left along Lime Street as it shrinks to a narrow corridor between Lloyd's and the Willis Building, with the sky almost shut out.

⓯ **Lloyd's** was built during 1978-86 by Richard Rogers and Partners. Famous for putting the facilities (lifts, toilets, etc) on the outside of the building to make way for the dramatic twelve-storey high atrium at the centre. The remarkable stainless steel structure of the exterior is particularly dramatic when floodlit.

Norman Foster and Partners designed the ⓰ **Willis Building** opposite, opened in 2008. It's 125m (410ft) tall with 26 storeys and 44,000sqm of floor space. The three curved sections have a stepped design, set back to provide the roof entertainment terraces, now seemingly mandatory on all new City buildings.

Completed in 2018, the Scalpel (official name) stands on the corner of Lime and Leadenhall Streets. With 38 storeys and 190m (620ft) tall, it was designed by Kohn Pedersen Fox. There's a basement restaurant, with a retail shop and café at street level.

The Scalpel

Emerge from Lime Street to cross Leadenhall Street onto an open piazza where you're surrounded by a surreal array of skyscrapers, plus two medieval churches which provide a connection with the real world.

The **⑰ Leadenhall Building**, designed by Rogers, Stirk, Harbour and Partners was completed in 2014. It's a simple, back-of-an-envelope design on a massive scale, 225m (738ft) high, with 48 floors. The vast ground floor entrance on Leadenhall Street has a huge wow factor.

The bravado building has a 10 degree cutback in order not to block the long view of St Paul's, which has inspired its 'Cheesegrater' nickname.

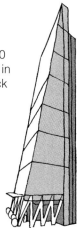

⑱ St Helen's was previously named The Aviva Tower or Commercial Union Building. Built in 1968-9 by Gollins, Melvin, Ward Partnership, it's 118m (387ft) tall with 28 floors. The tower overlooks a piazza, reminiscent of the USA, but its no nonsense, square box design looks dated next to its flamboyant neighbours.

However, plans were approved in 2016 to replace St Helen's with the Trellis Tower, a 310m (1017ft) high, 72-floor skyscraper, which will be the second-tallest building in the UK after the Shard. Aviva holds the present building's lease until 2024, so the new tower is not expected to be completed until some time in the late 2020s.

Lloyd's

Leadenhall Building

St Helen's

Across the piazza are the unmistakeable curves of ⑲ **30 St Mary Axe** (The Gherkin) built by Foster & Partners during 1997-2004. Short compared to the heights achieved by the lofty newcomers, the Gherkin is 'only' 195m (640ft) high, but its soft curvilinear shape makes it stand out from its mainly straight line neighbours.

The characteristic twisting effect is achieved by turning each of the forty floors through four degrees, giving the elevation a woven effect which has been likened to that of Argyle socks.

30 St Mary Axe became quickly accepted by Londoners and visitors as a building symbolic of the city and is now universally known by its affectionate nickname, 'The Gherkin'.

St Helen's Bishopsgate

St Andrew Undershaft and The Gherkin

⑳ **St Andrew Undershaft** dates back to 1520-32. Much restored over the years, it's remarkable as one of the few medieval churches to survive both the Great Fire and the bombs of World War II. Even the 17th-century stained glass in the west windows remains intact. The old church would be dull in another location but as an antidote to the glass monsters surrounding it the building is a quiet reminder of less bombastic times.

Dating from the 13th century, ㉑ **St Helen's Bishopsgate** also survived both the Great Fire and the Second World War. However, it sustained serious damage from IRA bombs in 1992-3 and was restored and reordered by architects Quinlan and Francis Terry.

The building we see today developed when local Benedictine nuns built a church alongside an existing 12th-century parish church, creating two separate places of worship. Over time it became one building but with two entrances and two naves, the northern one for the nuns and the southern for the laity. This has given the west end of the church the odd appearance of having two main entrances.

It's a remarkably peaceful spot in this manic location and, though now almost hidden amongst the thicket of shiny skyscrapers, is well worth seeking out along a footpath between St Mary Axe and Bishopsgate.

Continue along St Mary Axe and turn left into narrow Camomile Street. The Heron Tower soars above the right corner and the redeveloped 100 Bishopsgate site fills the left.

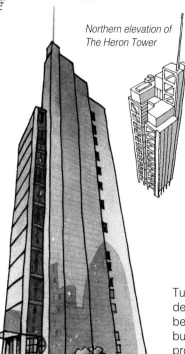

Northern elevation of The Heron Tower

The Heron Tower

The ㉒ **Heron Tower** was built 2002-11 by Kohn Pedersen Fox. Its 46 floors rise to 202m (663ft) plus the 28m (93ft) mast. A cluster of extruded rectangular tubes each with a different architectural treatment terminating at different heights gives the building a craggy silhouette.

Still not hemmed in by other towers, it benefits from space in front onto the open street. It's bulky, especially the northern elevation seen along Bishopsgate, but generally a standard office tower seemingly unconnected to City life, although there's an impressive aquarium in the entrance lobby and a public bar and restaurant on the top.

Turn left along Bishopsgate. The development of 100 Bishopsgate began in 2016 as a scheme of three buildings of 38, 16 and 6 storeys providing office, retail and restaurant space, completed in 2018.

Situated next to the building site, the small church of ㉓ **St Ethelburga** dates to the 13th century and has survived many changes, including rebuilds in the 15th century and another after an IRA bomb attack in 1993. The cheery little bell tower was added in 1775. The church is now a Centre for Reconciliation and Peace.

100 Bishopsgate rebuild

Demolition work for the building of 100 Bishopsgate revealed a view of St Ethelburga and beyond that's not usually seen.

Bishopsgate has been a main highway into London since Roman times and is named after one of the original eight gates in the London Wall. The coaching Inns that once lined the street, providing accommodation for travellers on the Old North Road, have now been mostly replaced by offices. A survey in 2011 found that though tens of thousands of people commute to and work in the area, it had a resident population of just 222!

Tower 42

99 Bishopsgate
104m (341ft) high.
25 office floors.
Completed 1976.

Gibson Hall

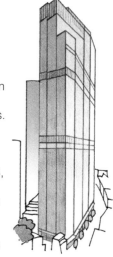

22 Bishopsgate

㉕ Gibson Hall, formerly National Westminster Bank and National Provincial Bank, stands where Bishopsgate joins Threadneedle Street. This richly decorated single-storey Corinthian pavilion, with statues on the roof and bas-relief panels of Victorian self-satisfaction, was built in 1865 by John Gibson who was responsible for a number of English banks. The building was converted to an events venue in 1981 and rebranded with the architect's name.

Beset by design and financial problems since 2008, 'The Pinnacle' was replaced by 22 Bishopsgate, a gargantuan office building more than twice the size of the City's biggest towers, rising to 278m (912ft) tall, just below the height of the Shard. The £1.5bn building is due for completion in 2019. Inescapable from every angle, you won't be able to miss it.

Further along Bishopsgate, **㉔ Tower 42** was formerly the National Westminster Tower, designed by Richard Seifert and built between 1970-81. It's 183m (600ft) tall with 47 floors and was Britain's tallest building when completed.

Still timelessly elegant, the tower was reclad and internally refurbished at a cost of £75 million after an IRA car bomb attack in 1993.

St Mary Woolnoth

Turn right, down narrow Threadneedle Street, then go left behind the Royal Exchange, passing a seated statue of George Peabody, an American banker and philanthropist.

Take the next right, along Cornhill where there's a statue of James Greathead, Chief Engineer of the City & South London Railway, who helped develop London's underground railways. The statue's plinth is actually a ventilation shaft for Bank station below.

At the end of Cornhill turn left into King William Street for a look at **㉖ St Mary Woolnoth**, built 1716-27 in Baroque style by Nicholas Hawksmoor. It's strikingly different to his other churches, with Corinthian columns supporting two flat-topped turrets from which something appears to be missing or has fallen off.

With this conundrum to contemplate we end our walk. Numerous entrances to Bank tube station are nearby.

WALK 13

The Tower to The Shard

Places of interest

❶ Trinity Square
❷ All Hallows by the Tower
❸ Tower of London
❹ Tower Bridge
❺ City Hall
❻ HMS Belfast
❼ Hay's Galleria
❽ The Shard
❾ Borough Market
❿ Southwark Cathedral
⓫ Southwark Gateway Needle
⓬ London Bridge
⓭ Fishmongers' Hall

— Route
▨ Prominent buildings
▨ Traffic-free
▨ Green areas
🚇 Tube station

START: Tower Hill tube station.
FINISH: Monument tube station.
LENGTH: 2 miles approx, mainly on traffic-free walkways. Flights of steps on and off the bridges.
REFRESHMENTS: The Tower, Tower Bridge, Hay's Galleria, Borough Market.

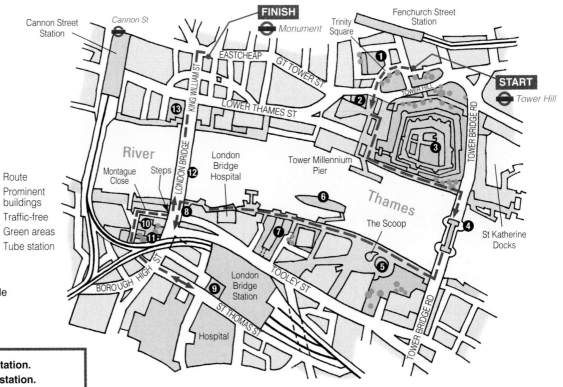

A short walk through a thousand years of history, from the 11th-century Tower of London to the 21st-century, glittering Shard. Between them cross the much-loved Victorian folly of Tower Bridge and end with a crossing of London Bridge. The views across the Thames to the City are spectacular. Note that this is prime tourist territory and you should expect crowds all the way.

THE WALK

Leave Tower Hill tube station by the Fenchurch Street exit into
❶ **Trinity Square**. The gardens on your left are where prisoners
from the Tower were executed. On the right is Trinity House,
headquarters of the 16th-century Trinity House Corporation which
is responsible for the lighthouses around the coasts of England and
Wales. The building, designed by Samual Wyatt and built in 1792-4,
boasts a sturdy Ionic façade and some fine interiors.

Ahead is the former Port of London Authority headquarters,
built in 1912 by Edwin Cooper, a monumental and extravagant
celebration of the London Docks, which once dominated world
trade. After the PLA moved to other premises in London the building
had various uses and in 2017 it was opened as a Four Seasons
luxury Hotel.

The Mercantile Marine Memorial in the gardens, designed by Sir
Edwin Lutyens, commemorates the men of the Merchant Navy and
fishing fleets who were killed in the two World Wars. The names of
12,000 dead are inscribed on bronze plaques.

*The former Port of
London Authority HQ*

Walk down the hill on the west side of the gardens (Trinity Square) and cross
busy Tower Hill road at the lights into the precincts of the Tower of London,
where griffins mark the boundary of the City of London.

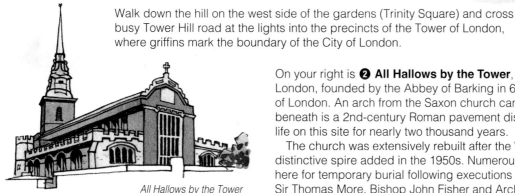

All Hallows by the Tower

On your right is ❷ **All Hallows by the Tower**, the oldest church in the City of
London, founded by the Abbey of Barking in 675AD, 300 years before the Tower
of London. An arch from the Saxon church can still be seen today. In the crypt
beneath is a 2nd-century Roman pavement discovered in 1926, evidence of city
life on this site for nearly two thousand years.

The church was extensively rebuilt after the World War II bombing, with the
distinctive spire added in the 1950s. Numerous beheaded bodies were brought
here for temporary burial following executions on Tower Hill, including those of
Sir Thomas More, Bishop John Fisher and Archbishop Laud.

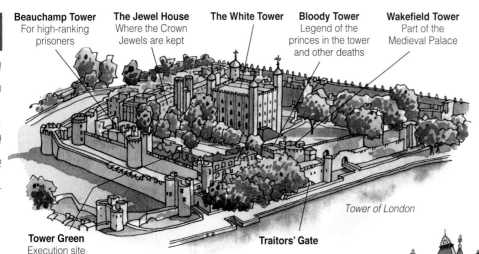

Beauchamp Tower
For high-ranking prisoners

The Jewel House
Where the Crown Jewels are kept

The White Tower

Bloody Tower
Legend of the princes in the tower and other deaths

Wakefield Tower
Part of the Medieval Palace

Tower of London

Tower Green
Execution site

Traitors' Gate

Begun by William the Conqueror around the 1070s, the ❸ **Tower of London** has been used for various purposes, including a royal residence, a much-feared prison and an execution site. The complex of several buildings is set within two concentric rings of defensive walls and a moat. There were major expansions in the 12th and 13th centuries but the layout today is much as it was 700 years ago.

The oldest part, the White Tower or the 'keep', was built as a residence for William I. He lived on the top floor, out of danger, with his court on the floors below. The walls are 4.6m (15ft) thick and 27m (90ft) tall, making the castle the tallest building in London at the time.

Walk down the hill past the Tower, turn left along the riverside and climb the steps onto Tower Bridge.

Designed by J Wolfe Barry, ❹ **Tower Bridge** was opened in 1894 after eight years of construction, quickly becoming a symbol for both English eccentricity and London itself. The twin towers are 65m (213ft) high with over 11,000 tons of steel providing the framework which was then clad in Cornish granite and Portland stone.

Built when tall ships used the river, the roadway was opened to let them through while the overhead section could still be used by pedestrians.

A four-year facelift of the bridge costing £4 million was completed in 2010, and a small timber-clad café-restaurant was added in 2012.

Tower Bridge

After admiring the panoramic views from Tower Bridge, descend the steps to City Hall, lounging on grassy Potters Field Park.

City Hall

Headquarters of the Greater London Authority (GLA), ❺ **City Hall** was designed by Sir Norman Foster and opened in July 2002, at a cost of £65 million. Its unusual, bulbous shape is intended to reduce the surface area and thus improve energy efficiency. The look of the edifice depends on where you're standing. From some angles City Hall looks terrific, from others it resembles a large, squashed pudding.

Next to City Hall is a sunken amphitheatre called The Scoop, which is used in the summer months for open-air performances.

Continue along the riverside walk, a wonderful traffic-free facility for rubber-necking walkers.

You pass ❻ **HMS Belfast**, launched at Belfast in 1938, the largest cruiser ever built for the Royal Navy. After service in World War II and further action during the Korean War the ship was retired in 1965 and opened as a museum in 1971.

HMS Belfast

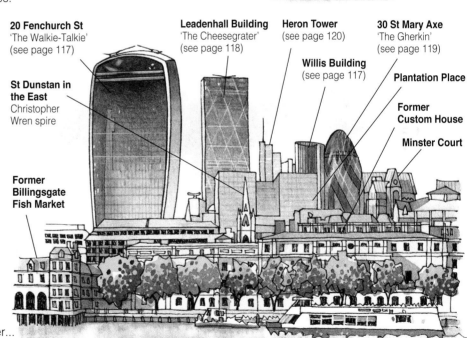

20 Fenchurch St
'The Walkie-Talkie'
(see page 117)

Leadenhall Building
'The Cheesegrater'
(see page 118)

Heron Tower
(see page 120)

30 St Mary Axe
'The Gherkin'
(see page 119)

St Dunstan in the East
Christopher
Wren spire

Willis Building
(see page 117)

Plantation Place

Former Custom House

Minster Court

Former Billingsgate Fish Market

As you continue along the riverside, the attention is irresistibly drawn to the panoramic view of the City across the river...

125

Hay's Galleria

Completed in 2012 and topping out at 310m (1,020ft) **❽ The Shard** is the tallest building in Western Europe. It was the brainchild of property developer, Irvine Sellar, and designed by Italian architect Renzo Piano, famously on the back of a menu during a meal with Sellar in a Berlin restaurant in 2000.

The spire-like tower, clad with 11,000 panes of glass, has 95 storeys, housing offices, a 2,000-bed hotel, apartments and observation platforms. Like most glass buildings it looks best when illuminated, either by sunlight or from inside, and its misaligned faces change colour with the weather. It also has a lightness lacking in many of the other London skyscrapers.

❼ Hay's Galleria was once an important wharf for tea clippers using its off-river dock. In a 1980s redevelopment the dock was filled in and a transparent roof added, while retaining much of the 1850s buildings.

It's now an elegant shopping and dining arcade with offices and living spaces above. A fountain at the centre of the Galleria is an animated 18m (60ft) bronze sculpture of a ship by David Kemp, unveiled in 1987.

Beyond Hay's Galleria a flight of steps climbs onto the approach to London Bridge. For a close-up view of the Shard turn left along Borough High Street then take the second on the left, St Thomas Street, to the base of the tower, where the monumental construction can be best appreciated.

The challenge was formidable. It was built on a ridiculously small site, over busy London Bridge railway station, across a narrow street from Guy's Hospital and close to London Bridge Hospital. Amazingly, during the three years of construction there was little disruption to any of their services.

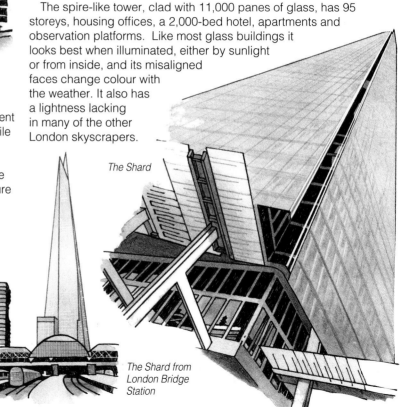

The Shard

The Shard from London Bridge Station

Retrace your steps and cross Borough High Street at the traffic lights to Bedale Street opposite.

Go under the railway viaduct into ❾ **Borough Market** which dates to the 11th century. Designed in 1851, today's building had an Art Deco entrance added in 1932 and further refurbishment in 2001. It's now a London institution, a fashonable place to shop for food, eat and drink, and a cheery place to explore, despite the tragic events of June 2017.

❿ **Southwark Cathedral** next door has been a place of Christian worship for over 1,000 years, but a cathedral only since 1905. Full of historic monuments and tombs, the present building is one of the capital's oldest Gothic churches, dating from around 1220 when it was part of a priory.

Southwark Cathedral

Walk around the cathedral perimeter on Montague Close. As it narrows, the arch of London Bridge is ahead, where a flight of steps on the left takes you up onto the bridge.

Southwark Gateway Needle

An odd-looking 16m (52ft) high stone spike, the ⓫ **Southwark Gateway Needle**, stands across the road, part of the regeneration plan for the area.

Since Roman times there have been various bridges over the Thames at this point, including the famous inhabited one built in 1176. The buildings were cleared in the late 18th century and its replacement, designed by John Rennie, was opened in 1831.

Increased heavy traffic eventually caused subsidence and the present ⓬ **London Bridge**, three spans of concrete box girders designed by architect Lord Holford, was completed in 1972. Rennie's bridge was sold to an American oilman, reassembled at Lake Havasu City, Arizona and re-dedicated in 1971.

Walk across the bridge from where there are fine views up and down the river. Snug on the north riverbank is ⓭ **Fishmongers' Hall**, an impeccable Greek revival, built in 1831-4 and designed by Henry Roberts. The Fishmongers, one of the City's oldest livery companies, was established in 1272. Company officials still fulfil their original role inspecting all fish sold in the City.

Continue straight on along King William Street to Monument tube station, the end of our walk.

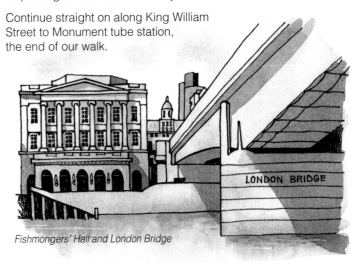

LONDON BRIDGE

Fishmongers' Hall and London Bridge

Some Architectural Terms

ARCADE A series of arches supporting a wall or set along it.

ART DECO Decorative style of bold geometric shapes and strong colours from 1920s to 1930s.

ART NOUVEAU Western European and American decorative style from end of 19th-century using plant-like, organic forms.

ARTS AND CRAFTS English decorative movement of late 19th century championing craftsmanship over mass production.

ATRIUM A central hall rising through the full height of a building with a glazed roof.

BAROQUE Ornate style of European architecture of the 17th and 18th centuries.

BAS-RELIEF Carving that stands out from the surface.

BRUTALIST Stark style of architecture especially of 1950s and 1960s using massive blocks of steel or concrete.

CAPITAL The broader section at the top of a pillar or column, often moulded.

CANTILEVER projecting support fixed at only one end.

CARYATID Stone carving of the female figure used as a pillar in Greek-style buildings.

CLASSICAL Influenced by ancient Greek or Roman forms or principles.

COLONNADE Row of evenly spaced columns supporting a roof, an entablature or arches.

CORNICE A horizontal moulded projection marking the top of a building or structure.

DORIC Classical column order with a plain capital.

ENTABLATURE The upper part of a classical building supported by columns or a colonnade.

FENESTRATION The arrangement and shape of window openings in a façade.

FLYING BUTTRESS a slanting support, typically forming an arch with the wall it supports.

GALLERY A long room or passage partly open at the side to form a portico or colonnade.

GEORGIAN Relating to reigns of British Kings George I-IV (1714-1830). Restrained elegance and use of neoclassical styles.

Philip Webb's 19 Lincoln's Inn Fields, (1868). An example of the use of a mixture of styles and influences

GOTHIC Originated in medieval western Europe using pointed arches and flying buttresses with large windows and elaborate tracery.

IONIC Classical column order with scrolls (volutes) on either side of the capital.

LANTERN Raised glazed area on top of a dome or roof to admit light.

MODERNISM European movement in the 1920s which rejected ornament for functionality.

PALAZZO A palatial building, especially in Italy.

PALLADIAN 18th-century English architecture in neoclassical style.

PAVILION Small free-standing building for occasional use.

PEDIMENT The triangular upper part of a classical building.

PILASTER A rectangular column projecting from a wall.

PERPENDICULAR 15th-century English Gothic with vertical tracery.

PORTICO A projecting entrance.

STUCCO Fine plaster for coating walls or moulding into decoration.

TRACERY Ornamental stone openwork, typically in the upper part of a Gothic window.

TRIBUNE a dias or rostrum, especially in a church.